THE
100+
SERIES™

Reproducible Activities

Reading Comprehension

Grades 1–2

Instructional Fair
An imprint of Carson-Dellosa Publishing LLC
Greensboro, North Carolina

Instructional Fair

Author: Holly Fitzgerald
Editor: Kathryn Wheeler

Instructional Fair
An imprint of Carson-Dellosa Publishing LLC
PO Box 35665
Greensboro, NC 27425 USA

ISBN 978-0-7424-1766-3
03-032128091

Table of Contents

Name _Mohammed_ Date _5/24/__

Ice Cream

Ice cream comes in many yummy flavors.

How do you make an ?

Dip a  of ice cream.

Put the  on the .

Eat your !

Ice cream is good on a hot day.

1. Put the steps in order. Write 1, 2, or 3.

___3___ Put the  on the .

___4___ Eat your .

___2___ Dip a  of ice cream.

2. Ice cream is good on a
   frati fikr
   _____ day.

3. Circle your favorite flavor.

chocolate   all

vanilla

strawberry

Name __Mohammed__   Date __5/24/2022__

The Bus

The bus takes people many places.

First the bus takes people to 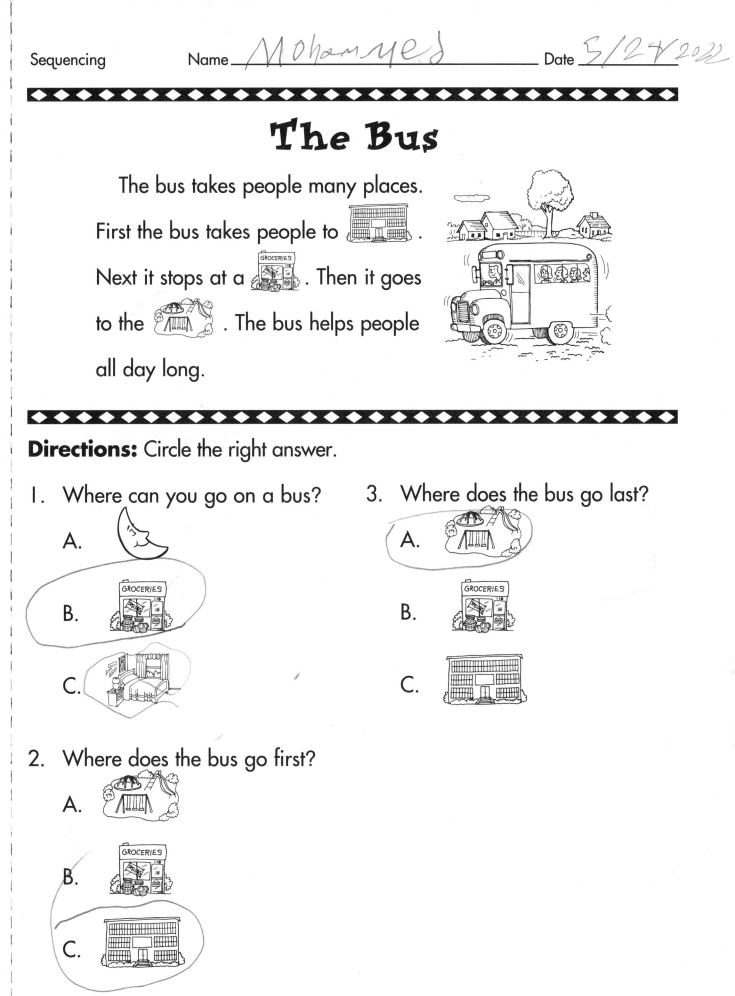 .

Next it stops at a 🏪 . Then it goes

to the 🛝 . The bus helps people

all day long.

Directions: Circle the right answer.

1. Where can you go on a bus?

    A. 🌙

    B. (circled)

    C.

2. Where does the bus go first?

    A.

    B.

    C. (circled)

3. Where does the bus go last?

    A. (circled)

    B.

    C.

5   0-7424-1766-2 • Reading Comprehension Grades 1-2

Trains

Trains ride on tracks. The 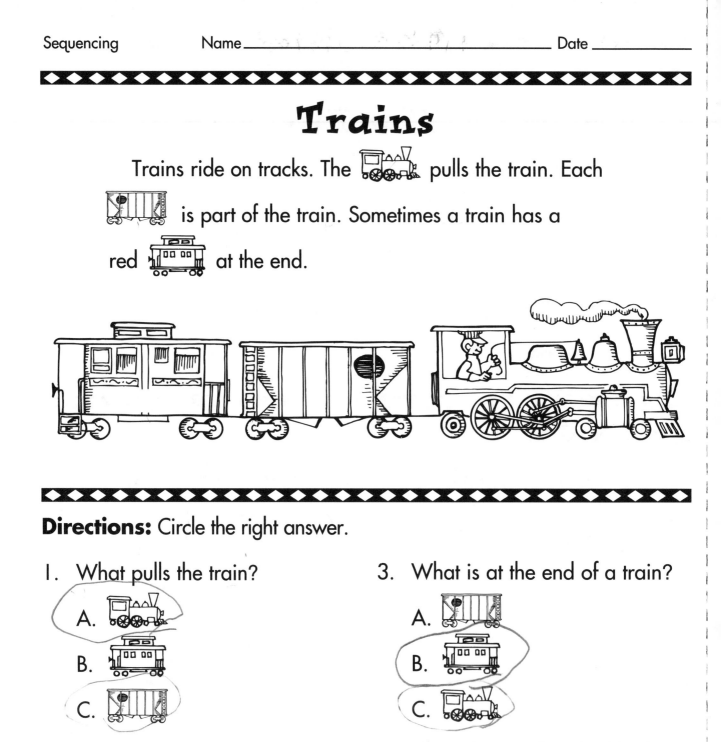 pulls the train. Each

is part of the train. Sometimes a train has a

red at the end.

Directions: Circle the right answer.

1. What pulls the train?

   A.

   B.

   C.

2. What comes next on the train?

   A.

   B.

   C.

3. What is at the end of a train?

   A.

   B.

   C.

4. Write the word in the blank.
   Trains ride on

   _____

   _ _ _ _ _ _ _ _ _ _ _ _ _

   _____ .

Days

There are seven days in a week. Sunday is the first day of the week. Saturday and Sunday are weekend days. The other five days are school days. Which day do you like best?

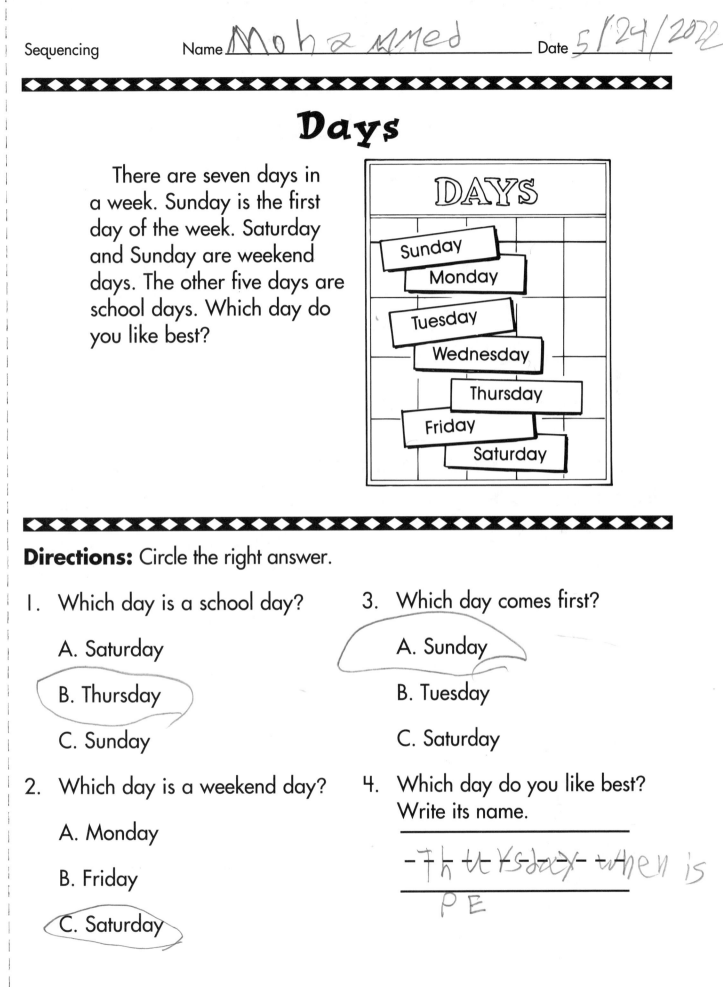

Directions: Circle the right answer.

1. Which day is a school day?

   A. Saturday

   B. Thursday

   C. Sunday

2. Which day is a weekend day?

   A. Monday

   B. Friday

   C. Saturday

3. Which day comes first?

   A. Sunday

   B. Tuesday

   C. Saturday

4. Which day do you like best? Write its name.

   Thursday when is PE

Name __Mohammed__   Date __5/24/20__

The Baseball Game

Bob and his dad go to a
baseball game. First, they sit
down. Then, Bob eats a 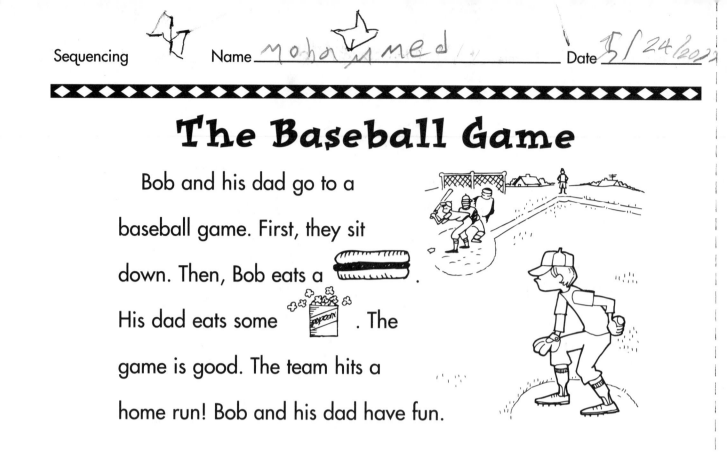.
His dad eats some 🍿. The
game is good. The team hits a
home run! Bob and his dad have fun.

Directions: Circle the right answer.

1. What did Bob and his dad do first?

   A. eat food

   B. hit a home run

   C. sit down

2. What did Bob eat?

   A. 🍿

   B.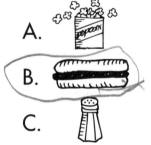

   C. 🧂

3. What happens in the baseball game?

   A. The team eats food.

   B. The team has fun.

   C. The team hits a home run.

4. Have you been to a baseball game?

   Yes   **No**

The Spider

A spider finds a good place for a home. She spins a web. She works hard. She waits for a fly. The fly will be her dinner.

Directions: Circle the right answer.

1. What does the spider do first?

    A. finds a good place for a home

    B. waits for a fly

    C. works hard

2. What does the spider do last?

    A. spins a web

    B. waits for a fly

    C. works hard

3. Do spiders have homes?

    Yes   **No**

4. Do spiders eat flies?

    Yes   **No**

5. Do spiders cook food?

    Yes   **No**

Penny

Penny is a pack rat.
She owns many things.
She has a hat, two baseball bats,
And three shiny rings.
Now Penny wants a new toy van,
A mouse trap, and a little fan!

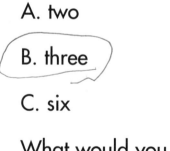

1. What does Penny own now?

    A. a new toy van

    B. a mouse trap

    C. two baseball bats

2. What does Penny want?

    A. a hat

    B. a little fan

    C. three rings

3. How many things does Penny own now?

    A. two

    B. three

    C. six

4. What would you like to own?

    _____

    _____

A Falling Star

Have you ever seen a falling star? Falling stars are not really stars. They are small pieces of rock. The rocks fall through the sky. They get hot and burn. The rocks look big because they give off light. That is why they are so bright. Another name for a falling star is a **meteor**.

1. Write 1, 2, and 3 to put the steps in order.

   _3_ The rocks look big because they give off light.

   _2_ The rocks fall through the sky.

   _1_ The rocks get hot and burn.

2. What is another name for a falling star?

   A. burning rock

   B. falling rock

   C. meteor

   D. night sky

3. Why do falling stars look so bright?

   A. because they are falling

   B. because they give off light

   C. because they are rocks

   D. because they are stars

Name MoHammed.   Date 5/24/2022

My Feelings

Today I had many feelings. I was happy when we had art class. I was sad when I heard a story about a hurt dog. When Gina took my pen, I was angry. When my brother yelled "Boo!" I was surprised.

Directions: What does each face show Draw a line.

1.    A. sad

2.   B. happy

3.   C. angry

4.   D. surprised

Directions: Circle the feeling from the story.

5. When we had art class, I was

   happy.   angry.

6. When I heard the story, I was

   surprised.   sad.

7. When Gina took my pen, I was

   happy.   angry.

8. When my brother yelled, I was

   surprised.   sad.

Name __MOHaMMed__ Date __5/24/2022__

Names

My name is Mary Ann
Brown. Everyone has a name.
My brother's first name is Jesse.
His middle name is William. His last
name is Brown. Our pets have names,
too. My cat is named Fluffy and my
fish is named Goldie. Even towns
have names! The name of our town is
Smithville. We used to live in Portland.

My name is
Mary Ann Brown.

Directions: Write in the chart. Use the Name Bank.

Name Bank					
Portland	Fluffy	Jesse	Smithville	Goldie	Mary

People Names	Pet Names	Town Names
Mary	Fluffy	Jesse
or	or	
Smithville	Goldie	Portland

Name _Mohammed_ Date _5/24/2026_

School

A school is a place where people go to learn. At school, students learn how to read. They learn how to spell new words. They learn math. They study science. Some schools also have lessons in art and music. A school can help you learn about many new things.

Directions: Look at the books. Draw a line from each book to its title.

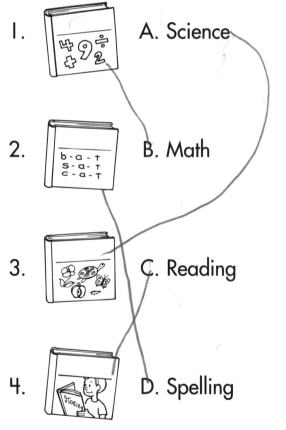

1. A. Science

2. B. Math

3. C. Reading

4. D. Spelling

5. What is your favorite subject in school?

science

6. What is the name of your school?

Alolham

ham

Fruits and Vegetables

Ang's mother sells fruit. Ang loves to look at the red apples and the yellow bananas. He likes the peaches, too. Ang's mother also sells vegetables. She sells carrots, corn, and potatoes. After school, Ang helps his mother at her store. He puts the fruits and vegetables into bags.

Directions: Look at the pictures. Write **F** next to each fruit. Write **V** next to each vegetable.

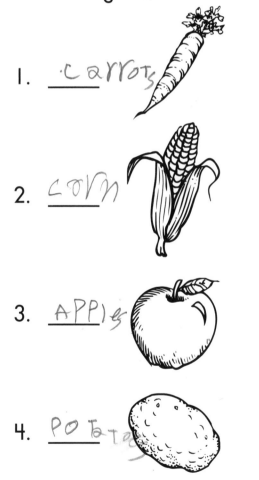

1. __carrots__

2. __corn__

3. __Apple__

4. __Potato__

5. __Peach__

6. Circle the picture of something that Ang's mother sells.

Name MOHAMMED   Date 5/24/2022

Baby Animals

Baby animals sometimes have special names. A baby cat is called a **kitten**. A baby horse is called a **colt**. A baby cow is a **calf**. A baby dog is a **puppy**. How many baby animal names do you know?

Directions: Draw a line from the name to the picture.

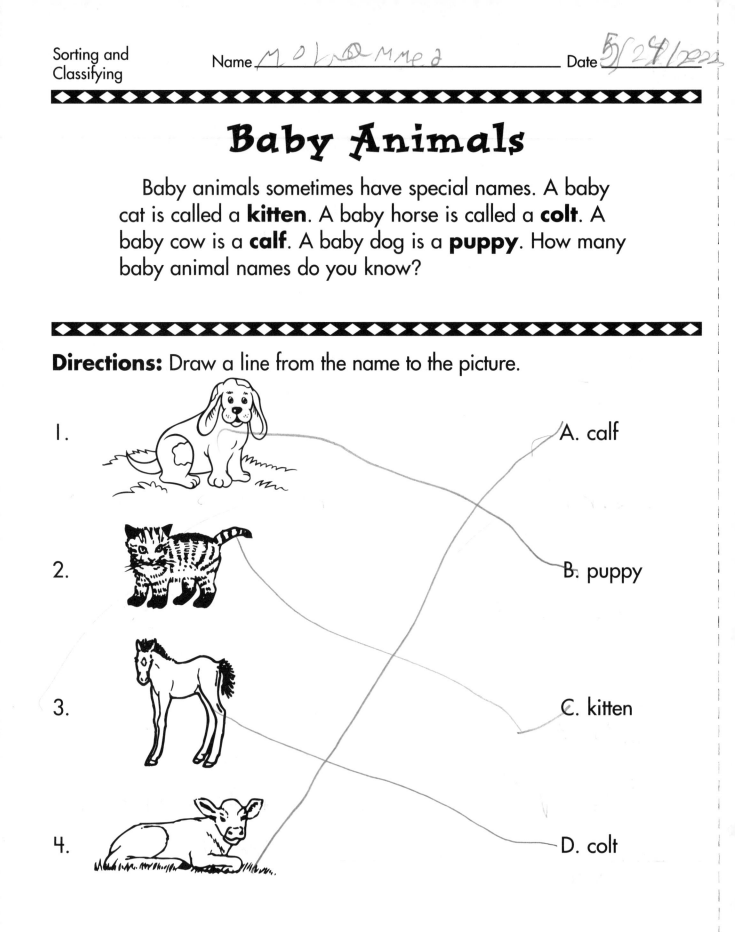

1.

2.

3.

4.

A. calf

B. puppy

C. kitten

D. colt

Name _Mohammed_ Date _5/24/2022_

All the Animals

There are many kinds of animals. Three kinds of animals
are mammals, birds, and reptiles.

Mammals have fur or hair. Baby mammals drink milk
from their mothers' bodies. A whale is a mammal.

Birds are the only animals that have feathers. A robin
is a bird.

Reptiles have scaly skin. Most reptiles lay eggs on the
ground. An alligator is a reptile.

Directions: Read each sentence.
Is it a mammal, a bird, or a reptile?
Write **M** for mammal. Write **B** for
bird. Write **R** for reptile.

1. __R__ Maggie brushes her hair.

2. __M__ The turtle lays its eggs in
the sand.

3. __B__ The blue jay has lost a
feather.

4. __B__ The piglets drink their
mother's milk.

5. __R__ A gull has white feathers.

6. __M__ The cat is cleaning
its fur.

Name _____mohammed_____ Date 5/28/2022

Months of the Year

There are twelve months in every year. March, April, and May are spring months. This is when flowers start to grow. June, July, and August are summer months. The weather is hot. It is fun to go to the beach. The fall months are September, October, and November. In some places, the leaves turn colors and the weather is cooler. December, January, and February are winter months. It is cold in these months.

Directions: Write the months in the chart.

Spring Months	Summer Months	Fall Months	Winter Months
March	weather	Seftnber	Januery
April	hot	ocTober	aug
May	fun	Novmber	febrnay

Name _Mohammed_ Date _5/26/202_

Shopping

Here are the stores on Main Street.

Directions: Read each shopping list. Where should each person shop? Write the store number.

1. John needs eggs, milk, and bread.
   Where should John shop

   Store Number __3__

2. Susie needs dog food and a bird cage.
   Where should Susie shop

   Store Number __5__

3. José needs gum drops, candy bars, and jellybeans.
   Where should José shop

   Store Number __4__

4. Chan needs two pieces of pizza.
   Where should Chan shop

   Store Number __2__

5. Sally needs nails and a hammer.
   Where should Sally shop

   Store Number __1__

6. Anna feels sick.
   Where should Anna shop

   Store Number __6__

Name _Mohammed_ Date _5/26/20_

Kites

Kites can fly
On windy days,
Up in the sky,
In the sun's rays.
My kite can dance
Across the blue;
I feel so glad
I could dance, too!

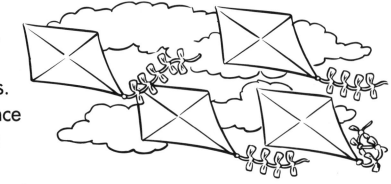

Directions: Circle the right answer.

1. What is the main idea of the poem?

   A. The sky is blue.

   B. I can run.

   C. Kites are fun.

2. Choose another title for this poem.

   A. The Sun's Rays

   B. Flying Kites

   C. Making Kites

3. What does "across the blue" mean?

   A. The kite is blue.

   B. The boy is sad.

   C. The sky is blue.

4. Write on the line. What color kite would you like?

   blue are Red and Green

◆◆◆◆◆◆◆◆◆◆◆◆◆◆◆◆◆◆◆◆◆◆◆◆◆◆◆◆◆◆

Way Out West

Jan spends her summers on her dad's ranch. Jan rides horses. She helps take care of the horses, too. She wears jeans, boots, and a cowboy hat. Jan loves the horses and cows. She loves the ranch.

◆◆◆◆◆◆◆◆◆◆◆◆◆◆◆◆◆◆◆◆◆◆◆◆◆◆◆◆◆◆

Directions: Circle the right answer.

1. This story is mainly about—

   A. Jan's summers on a ranch.

   B. Jan's riding lessons.

   C. Jan's school year.

   D. Jan's jeans and boots.

2. Another good title for this story is—

   A. "Jan's Horses."

   B. "Cows and Calves."

   C. "On the Ranch."

   D. "Summer."

3. Choose the words that tell about the main idea.

   A. jeans and boots

   B. horses and cows

   C. Jan and Dad

   D. ranch and summer

4. Circle the hat that Jan might wear on the ranch.

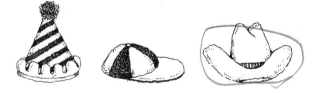

Name _Mohammed_ Date _5/06/202_

Letters

Letters, letters, all around!
They go from A to Z.
You use letters in your name
And for each word you see.
The letters of the alphabet
Are just like blocks for play.
You build your words
  with letters
And then read those words
  all day!

Directions: Write **T** for true or **F** for false.

1. __T__ The main idea of this poem is that letters make words.

2. __F__ Another good title for this poem is "Talking All Day."

3. __T__ Letters make names.

4. __F__ Letters are like building blocks.

5. Write your name.

   Mohammd

6. Write on the line. How many letters are in your name?

   Yes   T

Name Mohammed   Date 5/26/2022

Money

Money has been used for many years to pay for things. Most people are paid money for their jobs. They use the money to buy food, clothes, and other things they need. There are two kinds of money: **paper money** and **coins**. Before there was money, people would **trade** one thing for another. A farmer would trade eggs for cloth, or a horse for land. Money gives us an easy way to buy what we need.

Directions: Circle the right answer.

1. The main idea of this story is—

   A. how people pay for the things they need.

   B. how people get land for horses.

   C. how people work for money.

2. What did people do before there was money?

   A. They made their own money.

   B. They traded one thing for another.

   C. They went to the bank.

3. Which one of these is a trade?

   A. playing with toy cars

   B. giving a toy car for a bear

   C. having a car race

4. Which of these is a job?

   A. playing a game

   B. eating dinner

   C. teaching a class

Name _Mohammed_ Date _5/26/2022_

Snakes

There are many kinds of snakes. Some snakes are big and long. Some snakes are small. Snakes are **cold-blooded**. This means they need the sun or heat to stay warm. Snakes do not have legs. They crawl on the ground. Snakes cannot run, but they can move very quickly.

Directions: Write **T** for true or **F** for false.

1. __T__ The main idea of this story is to give facts about snakes.

2. __T__ Another good title for this story would be "All About Snakes."

3. __F__ Snakes cannot move.

4. __F__ All snakes are the same size.

5. __F__ This story tells how to take care of snakes.

Name _Mohammed_ Date _5/2/2022_

Sun Bears

A sun bear is the smallest of all bears. It is black with an orange circle on its chest. The orange mark looks like a sun. That is how the sun bear got its name. Sun bears have long claws. These claws help them climb trees. Unlike most bears, sun bears live in trees. They build nests out of sticks. These small bears sleep all day and hunt at night.

Directions: Write words in the blanks to complete the sentences.

1. This story is about
   Sun Bears
   _____ bears.

2. The _Are black_
   mark on the bear looks like the sun.

3. Sun bears use their claws to help them climb
   helP Tree.

4. Sun bears sleep all
   night .

5. Sun bears build
   nests
   out of sticks.

6. Sun bears hunt at
   night .

25   0-7424-1766-2 • Reading Comprehension Grades 1-2

Name _Mohammed_ Date _5/27/2002_

Hobbies

A hobby is something special that a person likes to do. Some people like to collect things as a hobby. They will buy or trade stamps, coins, or comic books. Some people enjoy sports as a hobby. They like to play baseball, tennis, or soccer. Some people build things as a hobby. People build model airplanes, chairs, or even houses. Other kinds of hobbies are reading, music, and raising pets. What is your hobby?

Directions: Write words in the blanks. Complete the sentences.

1. The main idea of this story is to tell about

   Hobbys .

2. Some people build

   model

   as a hobby.

3. Buying or trading

   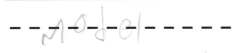
   is another kind of hobby

   is another kind of hobby.

4. A hobby is something special that a person

   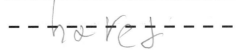
   hate

   to do.

5. Which hobby from the story would you like the best?

Name Mohammed Date 5/30/2021

Pets

The students in Mrs. Black's class talked about their pets.

Marla said, "My pet is Polly. She has green feathers. Her beak is sharp."

Rob said, "I keep my pet, Goldie, in a glass tank. She has a tail like a fan."

Nell said, "My pet, Slide, is long and thin. He slides along the ground."

Ang said, "My pet loves to wag his tail. His name is Sport."

Mrs. Black said, "Everyone has a great pet!"

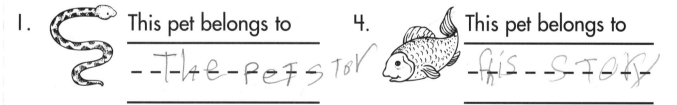

Directions: Write the name of each student next to his or her pet.

1. 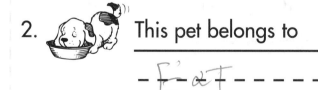 This pet belongs to
   The Pet Stor.

2. 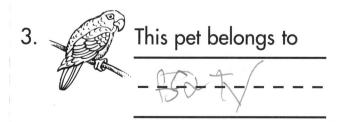 This pet belongs to
   Eat.

3. This pet belongs to
   Sort.

4. This pet belongs to
   his Story.

5. Circle another title for this story.

   A. "Pet Care"

   B. "Great Pets"

   C. "Dogs Are Best"

   D. "I Love Birds"

Name _Mohammed_   Date _5/30/22_

Birds

There are many kinds of birds. The bluebird is blue and orange. It can lay up to six eggs. The robin has a red breast. It lays three or four eggs. The cowbird is black and brown. The bald eagle is a large bird. It lays from one to four eggs. The hummingbird is a very small bird. Sometimes it has a red spot on its throat.

Directions: Draw a line. Match each bird to a detail that tells something about it.

1. bluebird
2. bald eagle
3. cowbird
4. hummingbird
5. robin

A. lays three or four eggs

B. blue and orange

C. large bird

D. black and brown

E. very small bird

Name: _Mohammed_   Date: _5/30/202_

The New Puppy

Chen has a new puppy named Ling at her house. Ling is tan. Chen loves the puppy's soft fur and big black nose.

"Ling is still a baby," Chen's mother says. "We need to feed her special food. She needs a warm bed, too."

"I want to pet and play with her all the time," says Chen.

"But sometimes you have to leave Ling alone," Chen's mother tells her. "She needs to rest and sleep. Soon Ling will want to play a lot of the time. But not yet."

Directions: Write in the web.

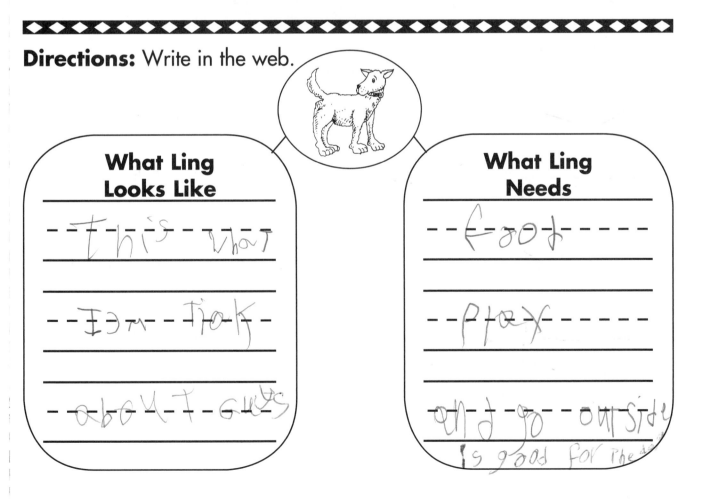

What Ling Looks Like

This what
I'm tak
about gues

What Ling Needs

food
play
and go outside
is good for the

◆◆◆◆◆◆◆◆◆◆◆◆◆◆◆◆◆◆◆◆◆◆◆◆◆◆◆◆◆◆◆◆◆◆

Stars

Do you see the stars at night? They shine in the sky. They look like tiny points of light. But stars are not small. Some stars are as large as our sun. Some stars are even bigger than our sun. Here on Earth the stars look very small to us. That is because they are so far away.

◆◆◆◆◆◆◆◆◆◆◆◆◆◆◆◆◆◆◆◆◆◆◆◆◆◆◆◆◆◆◆◆◆◆

Directions: Circle the right answer.

1. Some stars are—

    A. tiny points of light.

    B. as large as our sun.

    C. close to Earth.

    D. very dark.

2. Stars look small to us because—

    A. they are small.

    B. they are so far away.

    C. they shine so much.

    D. they are suns.

Directions: Write **T** for true or **F** for false.

3. Stars look like tiny points of light. ___T___

4. There are some stars that are bigger than our sun. ___F___

5. You can see stars at night. ___F___

6. Stars are close to us. ___F___

Name _____ Date _____

Starfish

Starfish live in the sea. But a starfish is not really a fish at all. It is an animal. It has tough, hard skin. This skin is covered with sharp bumps called **spines**. A starfish has five arms that make it look like a star. If one of these arms breaks off, the starfish can grow a new one. The mouth of the starfish is on the underside of its body.

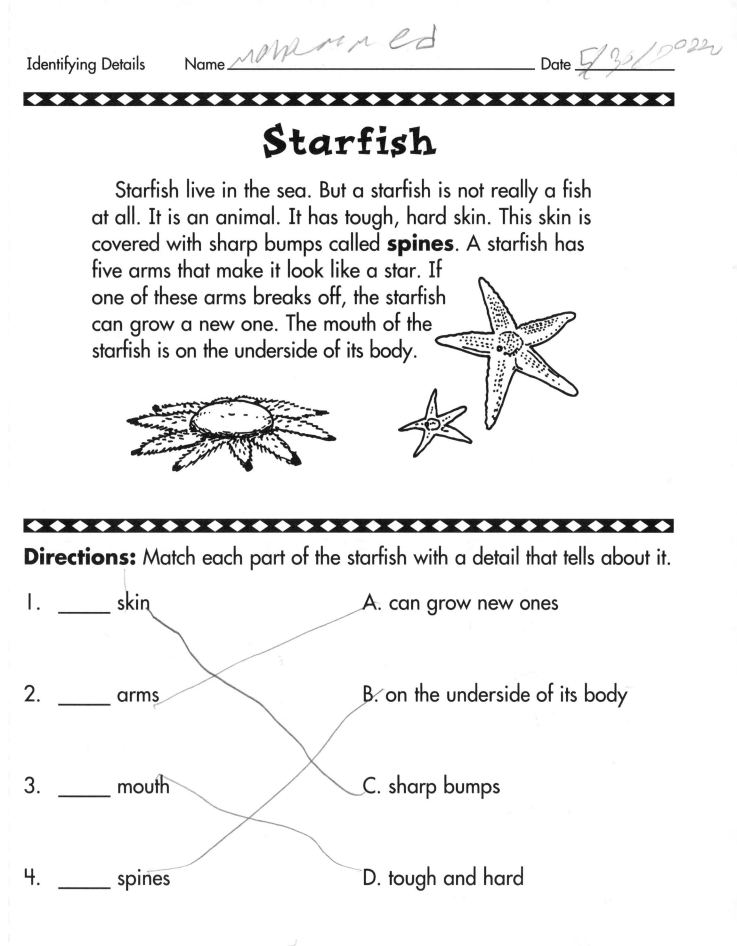

Directions: Match each part of the starfish with a detail that tells about it.

1. _____ skin   A. can grow new ones

2. _____ arms   B. on the underside of its body

3. _____ mouth   C. sharp bumps

4. _____ spines   D. tough and hard

A Letter to Juan

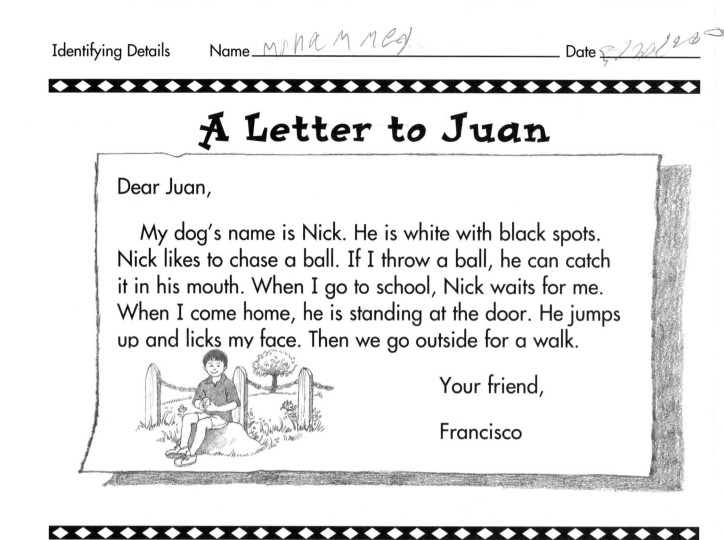

Dear Juan,

   My dog's name is Nick. He is white with black spots. Nick likes to chase a ball. If I throw a ball, he can catch it in his mouth. When I go to school, Nick waits for me. When I come home, he is standing at the door. He jumps up and licks my face. Then we go outside for a walk.

                              Your friend,

                              Francisco

1. Which dog is Nick?

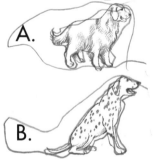

2. What detail helped you pick Nick?

    A. small with curly hair

    B. big with long, brown hair

    C. white with black spots

3. What trick can Nick do?

    A. He jumps up and licks faces.

    B. He goes for a walk.

    C. He can catch a ball in his mouth.

4. What do Nick and Francisco do after school?

    A. They chase balls.

    B. They go for a walk.

    C. They wait for school to end.

Name _Mohammed_ Date _8/30/2022_

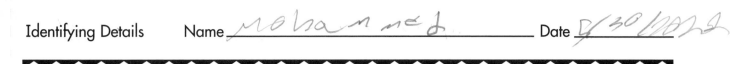

At the Mall

Lisa and her family are going to the mall. Dad wants to buy a new fan. Mom wants a vase for her flowers. John saved his money to buy a new toy truck. Lisa wants a red scarf. After they go shopping, the family will go out to dinner.

Directions: Write in the web. Write the name of each person below what he or she wants to buy.

Fan

truck

scarf

What They Want to Buy

vase

Fall

In the fall, the air gets cool. Students go back to school. Animals work hard to store food for the winter. Farmers store food, too. They harvest their crops. People work in their yards and rake leaves. In many places, the leaves turn red, yellow, and orange. It is a pretty time of the year.

Directions: Fill in the blanks to complete the sentences.

1. The air gets

   cool

   in the fall.

2. Animals work to store

   for the winter.

3. Farmers harvest their

   crops

4. People work in their

   orange

Name _Mohammed_   Date _6/30/08_

Maggie's Report

Maggie is writing a report. Her report is about Mount Rushmore. It is a mountain that is carved with the faces of four presidents. Read the sentences from Maggie's report. Cross out the ones that do not belong.

1. The faces of four presidents are carved into Mount Rushmore.

2. Pets cannot go to the park.

3. One of the faces is that of George Washington, our first president.

4. The other presidents on the mountain are Jefferson, Lincoln, and Roosevelt.

5. It is sunny a lot of the time.

6. The carvings help us remember great presidents.

Clouds

Do you know where rain comes from? Rain comes from the clouds in the sky. Clouds are made from water. That water falls out of the clouds as rain. Sometimes you can look at clouds and tell when it will rain. Clouds are white and puffy on sunny days. When it is going to rain, clouds turn gray.

Directions: Circle the right answer.

1. Choose the sentence that tells about the whole story.

   A. Clouds are white and puffy on sunny days.

   B. Rain comes from clouds in the sky.

   C. Clouds can be gray or black.

2. Clouds are—

   A. always white and puffy.

   B. gray on sunny days.

   C. gray when it is going to rain.

3. How can you tell if it is going to rain?

   A. from the water in the clouds

   B. from the sun

   C. from the color of the clouds

4. Circle the sentence that is true.

   A. Clouds are made of water.

   B. Rain comes from the air.

   C. Clouds are made of cotton.

Weather

Weather is what it is like outside. Weather is always changing. One day it may be hot. The next day, it may get cool. Sometimes it rains or snows. At other times, it may be foggy. Weather changes help us. When snow melts, it helps the ground get ready for new plants. Plants need both sun and rain to grow. Trees need cold weather to shed their leaves. Then they can grow new ones.

Directions: Circle the right answer.

1. Choose the sentence that tells about the whole story.

    A. Weather is always changing, and those changes help us.

    B. Weather is foggy in the spring.

    C. Weather needs to be cold for trees to grow.

2. Weather is—

    A. foggy and hot all the time.

    B. what it is like outside.

    C. what makes rain.

    D. always the same.

Directions: Write in the blank. Finish the sentence.

3. Rain, snow, and fog are all kinds

    of _sun_ .

4. _both sun and_ need
    both sun and rain to grow.

Name _Mohammed_ Date _8/30/2020_

Seals

Seals swim in the ocean. They come to land to rest. Seals have shiny fur. They have big, dark eyes. Seals can see well under the water. Their favorite food is fish. Seals do not chew their food. They can eat a whole fish in one big gulp!

Directions: Circle **Yes** or **No**.

1. This story is about seals and how they live.

   Yes   **No**

2. Seals like to eat grass.

   Yes   **No**

3. Seals can see well under the water.

   Yes   **No**

4. Seals chew their food.

   Yes   **No**

A Rabbit Poem

The rabbit is small and fast,
With a short and fluffy tail.
He has long ears that let
  him hear
Scary animals without fail.
Rabbits love to eat and eat!
They love the green,
  green grass.
They love to munch on vegetables
In a farmer's garden patch.

Directions: Answer the questions. Be sure to write complete sentences.

1. Write a sentence that tells about the whole poem.

   Sun you is his

   power sun is so

2. Write a sentence to tell what rabbits look like.

   stroger he with

   at the one star from

The Earth

Earth is a planet. It revolves around the sun. This planet has everything we need to live. Earth has land and water. It gets light and heat from the sun. The heat keeps us warm. The light helps plants to grow. We breathe the air that surrounds Earth. We can grow food here. Earth is a good home.

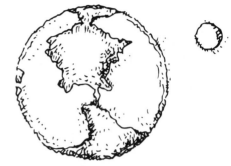

1. Earth is a—

   A. sun.

   B. country.

   C. planet.

   D. land.

2. This story tells us—

   A. why Earth is a good home for us.

   B. how Earth revolves around the moon.

   C. why Earth has air.

   D. how Earth makes heat for itself.

3. How does Earth get its light and heat?

   A. from the air

   B. from water

   C. from land

   D. from the sun

4. What are two important things that Earth gives us?

   A. air and water

   B. land and rocks

   C. light and heat

   D. toys and games

Football

Football is a fun game to watch or play. Players wear special uniforms. They wear pads to protect their bodies. They wear helmets to protect their heads. A football game is played with two teams. Each team tries to make a touchdown. Some players are good runners. Others can throw the ball well. It takes the whole team to win a football game.

Directions: Answer the questions. Be sure to write complete sentences.

1. Write a sentence that tells about the whole story.

   feet   Beet   is

   so   food   I Love

2. What does it take to win a football game?

   feet   players   foutbl

   down

Name Mohammed   Date 5/25/2002

Nelly Bly

Nelly Bly wanted to work for a newspaper. But in 1885, many people thought that women could not do this job. She did not give up. Finally she met a man who could give her a job. She proved to him that she could write good stories for his newspaper. She got the job! Nelly became well known as a **reporter**, someone who writes for a newspaper.

1. Which sentence tells about the whole story

    A. Nelly Bly was a good writer.

    B. Nelly Bly did not give up, and she got her dream job.

    C. Nelly Bly did not think that women could write for newspapers.

2. Why was it hard for Nelly to get a job as a reporter

    A. Because in 1885, many people thought that women could not do this job.

    B. Because in 1885, many women worked for newspapers.

    C. Because in 1885, many people were out of work.

3. What is a reporter

    A. someone who teaches report writing

    B. someone who writes for a newspaper

    C. someone who counts money for a bank

Big Dogs, Little Dogs

If you are getting a dog, you need to choose between a big dog and a little dog. Both dogs can make great pets. Both dogs can be good friends. But there are differences between big dogs and little dogs.

A little dog can sit on your lap. It can live indoors and does not take up much space. Sometimes, a little dog can be noisy. Small dogs need to be trained not to bark too much.

A big dog may have to live outside. It will need more food and more space. Big dogs can guard your house. They can help you stay safe.

Directions: Write in the Venn diagram. Compare little dogs and big dogs.

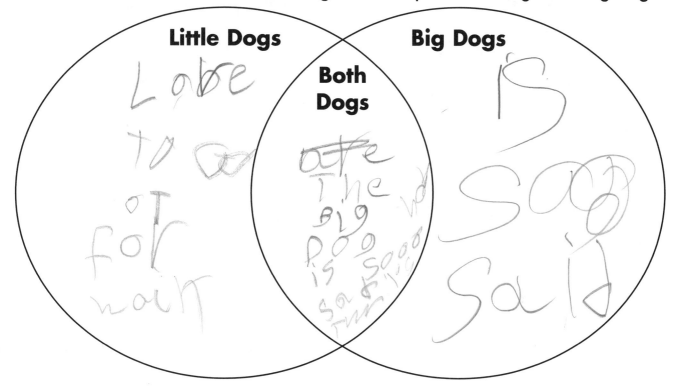

Winter Fun

Winter can be cold and snowy. People need to wear hats, coats, boots, and mittens to keep warm. In winter, it is fun to make snowmen. You need a carrot when you make your snowman. You also need coal or buttons. You can use a hat and a scarf to dress up your snowman.

Directions: Circle the right answer. Use the picture to help you.

1. Why do people need to wear mittens in winter?

   A. to keep their heads warm

   B. to keep their hands warm

   C. to keep their toes warm

2. Why do you need a carrot to make a snowman?

   A. to make hands

   B. to make eyes

   C. to make a nose

3. Why do you need coal or buttons to make a snowman?

   A. to make a nose and buttons

   B. to make the eyes and buttons

   C. to make fingers and toes

4. Draw a hat on the snowman in the picture. Color the hat.

Name __Mohammed__   Date __5/25/200x__

Snow

Snow is small, white flakes of frozen water. Snow falls to the ground when the air is cold. If the ground is warm, the snow **melts**, or turns back into water. If the ground is cold, snow stays on the ground.

When a lot of snowflakes fall quickly, it is called a **snowstorm**. A **blizzard** is a snowstorm when the wind blows hard. During a blizzard, snow can end up in big piles called **snow drifts**.

Directions: Write **T** for true or **F** for false.

1. __F__ Snow is small flakes of frozen water.

2. __F__ When snow melts, it freezes.

3. __T__ When a lot of snow falls, it is called a snow drift.

4. __T__ A blizzard is a snowstorm when the wind blows hard.

5. __F__ Snow melts if the ground is warm.

6. __F__ When snow falls quickly, it is called melting.

                   0-7424-1766-2 • Reading Comprehension Grades 1-2

Parks

A park is a place for people to enjoy the outdoors. Most parks have lots of trees and flowers. People can sit on benches and enjoy the view. Children who come to the park can play on swings and slides. Sometimes people bring food to a park and eat at picnic tables. Parks are fun to visit.

Directions: Match the words to the pictures. Draw lines.

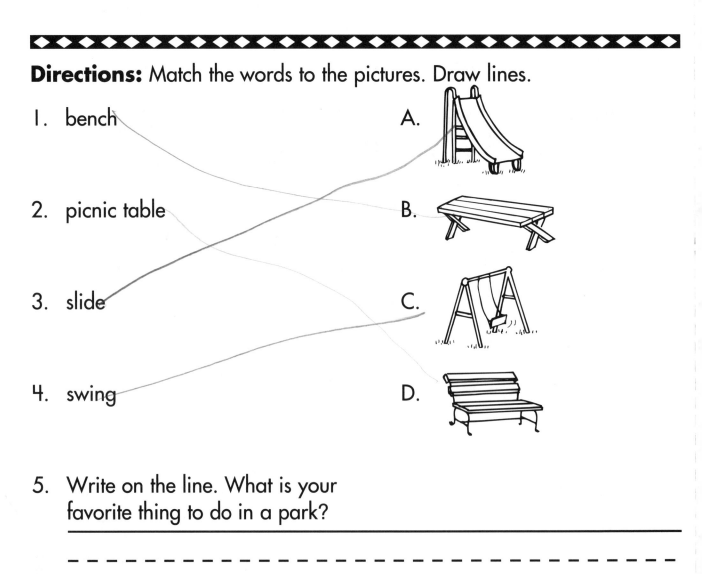

1. bench

2. picnic table

3. slide

4. swing

A.

B.

C.

D.

5. Write on the line. What is your favorite thing to do in a park?

_____

– – – – – – – – – – – – – – – – – –

_____

Name _M̲o̲M̲M̲R̲u̲u̲ ̲e̲d̲_____ Date _5̲/̲2̲8̲/̲2̲0̲2̲2̲_

Bike Safety

No matter how old you are, there are rules to follow when you ride your bike. These rules keep bike riders safe. Riding a bike should be fun, but it is also important to know the rules.

Directions: Match each safety rule with a picture. Draw a line.

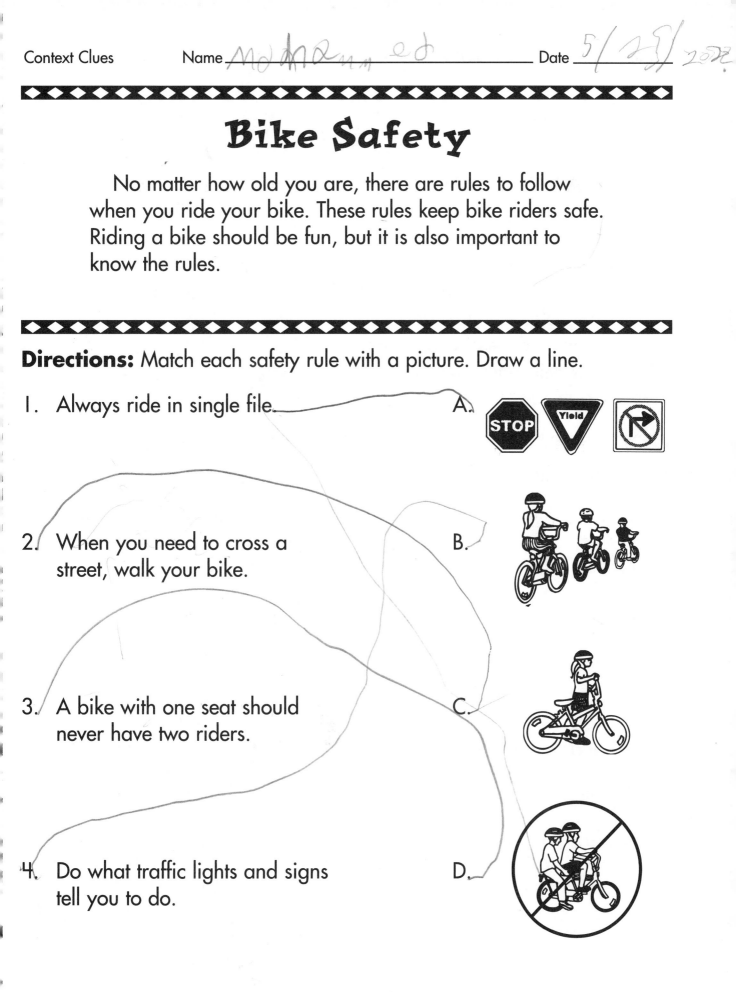

1. Always ride in single file.

   A.

2. When you need to cross a street, walk your bike.

   B.

3. A bike with one seat should never have two riders.

   C.

4. Do what traffic lights and signs tell you to do.

   D.

Foxes

A fox looks a little like a dog. It has a pointed **snout** or nose, big ears, and a bushy tail. Foxes often live in **burrows**, or holes in the ground. They hunt at night. They use their **senses**, such as sight, smell, and hearing, to help them hunt. Foxes eat **rodents** such as mice and squirrels. They also eat birds and frogs. Foxes are **clever**, or smart. This helps them live in the wild.

Directions: Circle the right answer.

1. What is a **snout**?

   A. ears

   B. tail

   C. nose

   D. paws

2. What does **clever** mean?

   A. wild

   B. smart

   C. fast

   D. hunter

3. Which one of these is a **rodent**?

   A. a frog

   B. a bird

   C. a cat

   D. a mouse

4. What is a **burrow**?

   A. a hole in the ground

   B. a kind of nose

   C. a tree branch

   D. a kind of animal

The Days Grow Short

Joe watched a busy little **mammal** climb up the tree. Then it raced down again, looking for nuts. Joe knew that it was **hoarding** nuts, storing them for winter. The animal came back with an **acorn** in its mouth. "It found another nut!" thought Joe. "That little guy will be **prepared** when winter comes."

Directions: Circle the right answer.

1. What is the mammal that Joe is watching?

   A. a squirrel

   B. a cat

   C. a mouse

   D. a dog

2. What does **hoarding** mean?

   A. eating

   B. racing

   C. storing

   D. climbing

3. What is an **acorn**?

   A. a mammal

   B. a kind of nut

   C. a kind of tree

   D. a season

4. What does **prepared** mean?

   A. warm

   B. hungry

   C. fast

   D. ready

All Kinds of Boats

There are many kinds of boats. A **rowboat** is a small boat that is moved with oars. **Oars** are long poles with wide, flat ends. A **tugboat** is a small, strong boat. It can push or pull boats that are much bigger. Another kind of boat is a **fireboat**. It puts out fires with water and hoses. A **sailboat** is moved by the wind. It has sails, which are made from strong cloth. The wind fills the sails and moves the boat through the water. A **houseboat** is a wide, flat boat with rooms where people can live.

Directions: Write the correct answers to the riddles.

1. I am moved by the wind. What am I?

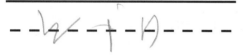

2. I help put out fires. What am I?

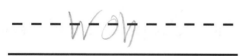

3. I am moved with oars. What am I?

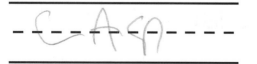

4. People can live in my rooms. What am I?

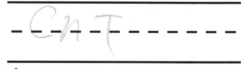

5. What kind of boat is this?

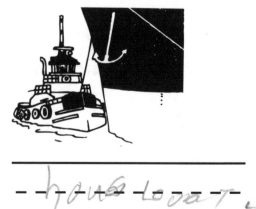

houseboat

The Rodeo

Jason and his dad went to a **rodeo**. A rodeo is a show for cowboys and cowgirls. One event is the **bucking horse contest**, where riders try to stay on wild horses for as long as they can. Another contest is **calf roping**. In this contest, a cowboy tries to rope and tie a calf's legs. There is also **bareback riding**, where a horse is ridden without a saddle. Prizes are given for each event. Jason said, "A rodeo is fun to watch!"

Directions: Draw lines to match each word to its meaning.

1. rodeo

2. bucking horse contest

3. bareback riding

4. calf roping

A. tying a calf's legs

B. riding without a saddle

C. riding a wild horse

D. a show for cowboys and cowgirls

Compare
and Contrast

Name _Mohammed_   Date _5/25_

Too Hot! Too Cold!

Sometimes we feel too hot or too cold. When it is cold
outside, we need to wear coats and boots to keep warm.
When it is hot outside, we can go swimming or drink
lemonade. There are many things we can do to feel better
when we are too hot or too cold.

Directions: Circle the words **too hot** or **too cold** to finish each sentence.

1. I put on a ☐ if I feel

    too hot.   (too cold.)

2. I turn on a ☐ if I feel

    too hot.   (too cold.)

3. I sit under a ☐ when I feel

    too hot.   (too cold.)

4. I put on my ☐ when I feel

    too hot.   (too cold.)

5. I drink cold ☐ when I feel

    too hot.   (too cold.)

6. I wear a ☐ when I feel

    too hot.   (too cold.)

Name _Mohammed_   Date _____

Dinosaurs

Dinosaurs lived a long time ago. They were very big animals. Some dinosaurs ate meat. Other dinosaurs ate plants. Most dinosaurs walked across the ground. A few dinosaurs could fly.

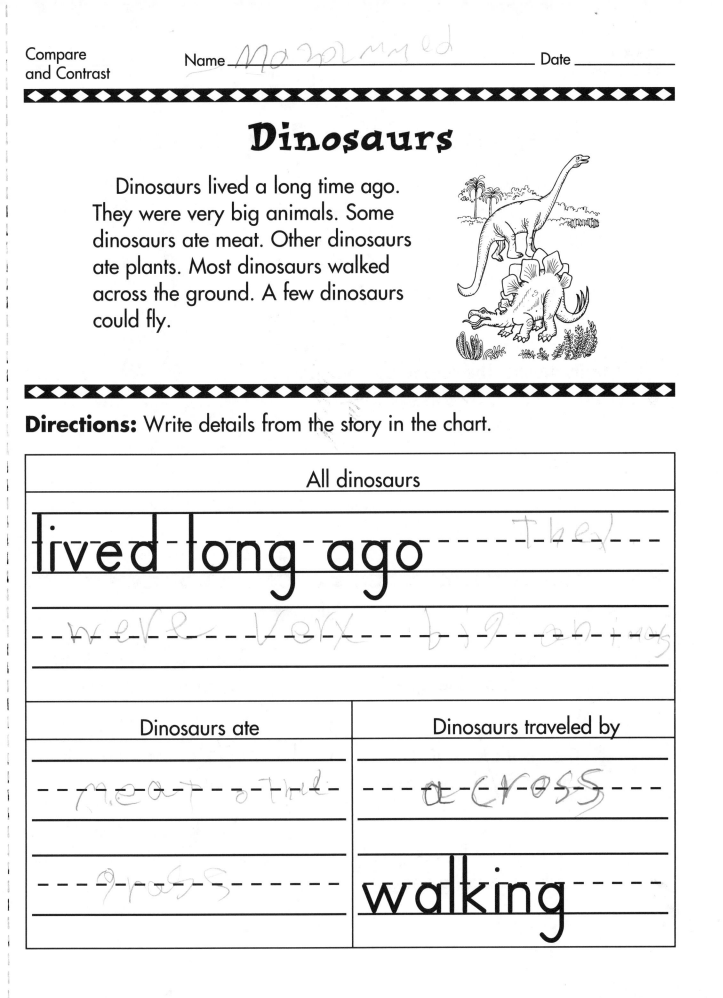

Directions: Write details from the story in the chart.

All dinosaurs
lived long ago   They
were very big animals

Dinosaurs ate	Dinosaurs traveled by
meat the	across
grass	walking

Elephants and Giraffes

Elephants and giraffes are alike because they are mammals. They are different in many other ways. One animal has a long trunk and the other has a long neck. Both animals look for food, but they eat differently. The elephant uses its long trunk to pick up food and put the food in its mouth. The giraffe can eat leaves from tall trees because of its long neck and legs.

Directions: Write **T** for true or **F** for false.

1. __T__ The elephant is a mammal, but the giraffe is not.

2. __T__ The giraffe uses its long neck to reach for leaves in trees.

3. __F__ The elephant has a long trunk and a long neck.

4. __T__ The giraffe has a long neck and long legs.

5. __F__ The elephant uses its trunk to put food in its mouth.

6. __T__ The elephant looks for food, but the giraffe does not.

Name ___Mohammed___ Date ___8/17/22___

Time

There are many ways that we measure time. A year is made of 365 days. A week has 7 days. One day is made up of 24 hours. Each hour is 60 minutes. One minute is made up of 60 seconds. How short is 1 second? You can blink your eyes 1 time in 1 second.

Directions: Circle the right answer.

1. Which is the longest?

    A. a week

    B. an hour

    C. a minute

    D. a second

2. Which is the shortest?

    A. a year

    B. a day

    C. a week

    D. a minute

3. Which is the longest?

    A. 5 weeks

    B. 5 days

    C. 5 minutes

    D. 5 seconds

4. Which is the shortest?

    A. 365 days

    B. 365 minutes

    C. 365 seconds

    D. 365 years

Name _mohammed_ Date _8/_

Penguins and Robins

Who loves the cold Penguins, that's who!
They dive and they swim right under the ice.
Robins go south when the warm weather stops,
And they don't fly back north until it is nice.
Penguins can't fly, but robins can soar.
They fly up to the clouds and back to their nest.
The black-and-white penguin waddles on snow,
And if it gets tired, it can slide for a rest!

Directions: Circle the right answer.

1. Who loves the cold weather?

   A. penguins

   B. robins

2. Which birds fly?

   A. penguins

   B. robins

3. Which birds can swim?

   A. penguins

   B. robins

4. Who flies south when it gets cold?

   A. penguins

   B. robins

Wolves

Chung tells her little sister, Ana, about wolves.

"Dog!" says Ana, pointing at the wolf picture.

"It is a wolf, not a dog," says Chung. "But dogs and wolves look alike. They are from the same animal family. A wolf can bark, just like a dog."

Ana points to the wolf's fur. "Soft," she says.

Chung nods. "That's right. The wolf has soft, thick fur. It helps keep him warm. Wolves go hunting at night. Dogs are awake during the day. But both wolves and dogs eat meat."

Directions: Write **T** for true or **F** for false.

1. __T__ Wolves and dogs can both bark.

2. __F__ Dogs are awake during the day.

3. __F__ Wolves go hunting during the day.

4. __F__ Wolves eat meat, but dogs do not.

5. __T__ Wolves and dogs are from the same animal family.

Map Facts

Amy, Pam, Miguel, and Clay all live in the same neighborhood. Look at the map and find their houses.

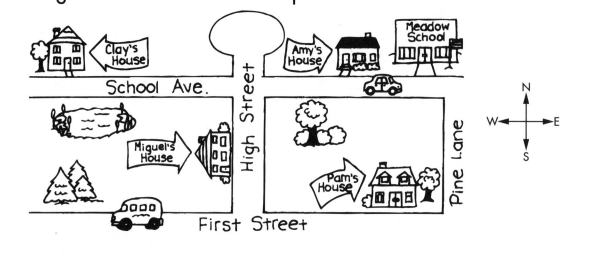

Directions: Answer the questions about the map.

1. Which girl lives closer to the school?

   A. Amy

   B. Pam

2. Whose house does not sit on a street that goes left to right?

   A. Miguel

   B. Pam

3. Whose house has the most windows?

   A. Amy

   B. Miguel

4. Who lives farther north?

   A. Clay

   B. Miguel

5. Who lives farther south?

   A. Amy

   B. Pam

Name _____ Date _____

Zoo Riddles

Josh the zookeeper has to paint new signs for the zoo. Josh has decided to make his chore into a game. He has made up a riddle about each animal.

Directions: Read the riddle. Write the name of the animal on the line. Use the Word Bank to help you.

Word Bank			
zebra	giraffe	lion	seal

1. I look like a horse, but I'm black and white.
   If you tried to ride me, I would give you a fright!

   _____

   - - - - - - - - - - - - -

   _____

2. I have a very loud roar and a mane.
   I am the king—I think that is plain.

   _____

   - - - - - - - - - - - - -

   _____

3. I dive and swim, catch fish, and bark.
   My fur is shiny and very dark.

   _____

   - - - - - - - - - - - - -

   _____

4. When I am hungry, I don't have to peck.
   I just reach to the trees with my long neck.

   _____

   - - - - - - - - - - - - -

   _____

The Sun

The sun is a big star. Earth is closer to the sun than to other stars. Because it is close, the sun gives us light. It keeps us warm.

The light and warmth of the sun also help plants to grow. It is fun to fish on a sunny day.

Directions: Write the words to finish the sentences.

1. The _____ is a big star.

2. Because the sun is close, it _____ us light.

3. The light of the sun also keeps us _____.

4. Draw a sun in the picture. Color it yellow.

Traffic Signs

Traffic signs keep you safe. Some signs tell you to stop.
Some signs tell you to go. When you do what the signs
say, you stay safe. You help keep other people safe, too.

Directions: Show what each sign tells you to do. Write **Stop** or **Go**
next to each picture.

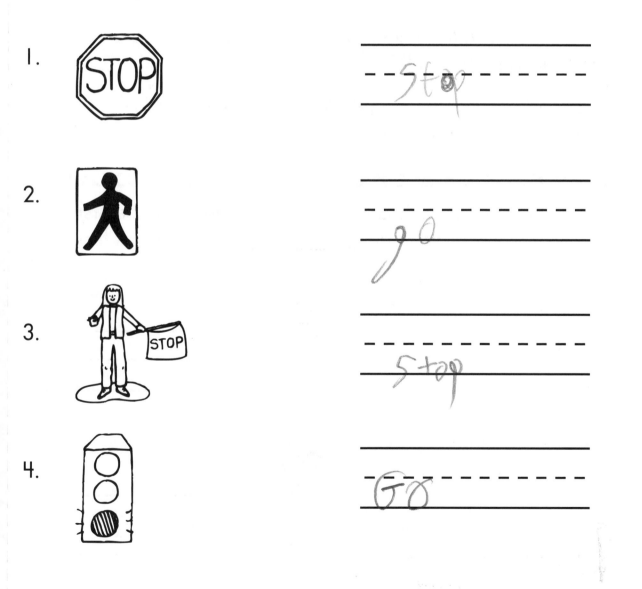

1. _____ Stop _____

2. _____ go _____

3. _____ Stop _____

4. _____ Go _____

Who Is First?

On Monday, Ms. Perez said, "The tallest student will be first in line."

On Tuesday, Ms. Perez said, "The shortest student will be first in line."

On Wednesday, Ms. Perez said, "The student wearing a dress will be first in line."

On Thursday, Ms. Perez said, "The student wearing a shirt with a number will be first in line."

On Friday, Ms. Perez said, "The student wearing his shirt tucked in will be first in line."

Directions: Ms. Perez's words caused a different student to be first in line each day. Write the correct day on which each student was first.

Wonderful Wheels

Did you ever think how it would feel
If nobody had invented the wheel
No bikes, no wagons, no trucks or trains,
No cars to ride … not even planes!
Life would really be a bore
If wonderful wheels were no more.

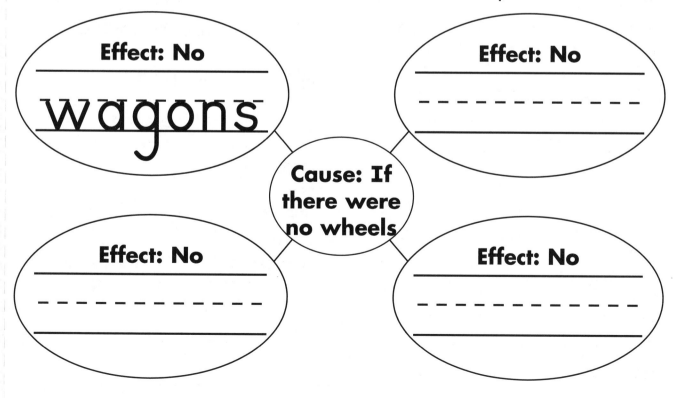

Directions: Write in the web. Write words from the poem.

Effect: No

wagons

Effect: No

Cause: If there were no wheels

Effect: No

Effect: No

Recycling

Dear Angela,

    In my family, we recycle. That means we put our trash into three bins. Plastic goes into one bin. Glass and cans go into another bin. Paper goes into the last bin. When the trash is taken away, it can be made into new things. I think this is the best way to take care of trash. If we put trash into the ground or into the sea, it will hurt the earth.

            Your pen pal,

            Maria

1. To recycle, Maria's family—

   A. puts trash in the ground.

   B. puts trash into three bins.

   C. puts trash in the sea.

2. Recycled trash—

   A. is made into new things.

   B. is thrown away.

   C. is put in one big bin.

3. If we put trash into the ground or the sea—

   A. it will make the earth better.

   B. it will make paper.

   C. it will hurt the earth.

4. Fill in the chart.

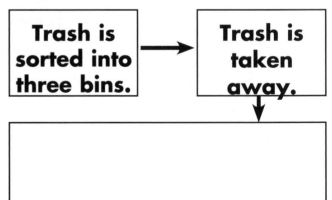

Humpty Dumpty

Humpty Dumpty rode by a wall.
His horse tripped and made him fall.
On his way down, Humpty hit his
    head hard.
Could he be hurt? Friends ran
    to the yard.
But Humpty was fine. "I'm
    not hurt," he said.
"I wear a hard helmet on my
    egg head."

Directions: Connect each cause and effect. Draw a line.

1. Friends ran to the yard

2. Humpty was not hurt

3. Humpty fell

A. because his horse tripped.

B. because they wanted to see if Humpty was hurt.

C. because he wore a helmet.

◆◇◆

Animal Team Work

Animals can work in teams. Some small fish eat food from the teeth of big fish. Then the big fish have clean teeth! Ants can get food from some small bugs. Then the ants keep the small bugs safe from other bugs. There are other animals that keep each other safe. One animal eats while the other animal keeps watch. They take turns eating. Animal teams can work well together.

◆◇◆

Directions: Draw lines to match each cause to the effect.

1. A small fish eats food from the teeth of big fish.

   A. They take turns eating and stay safe.

2. Ants get food from small bugs.

   B. Small bugs are kept safe by ants.

3. Animals take turns keeping watch.

   C. The big fish has clean teeth.

_____

4. Write on the line. When have you been part of a team?

   _____

   _

   _____

Hummingbirds

Hummingbirds are the smallest birds in the world. They are also very fast. A hummingbird flaps its wings 50 times every second! The wings flap so fast that they make a humming sound. That is where the bird gets its name. Hummingbirds must eat every 10 minutes. A hummingbird's heart beats very fast. It needs a lot of energy from food just to keep its heart beating to stay alive. A hummingbird's beak is long and pointed so it can drink sugar from the centers of flowers.

Directions: Circle the right answer.

1. The hum of a hummingbird's wings is—

    A. because of its beak being long.

    B. because of how fast it flaps its wings.

    C. because it is in a hurry.

2. A hummingbird must eat every 10 minutes—

    A. because it needs energy to stay alive.

    B. because it is not hungry.

    C. because it is so small.

3. A hummingbird can drink sugar from flowers—

    A. because it flies so fast.

    B. because it has a fast heartbeat.

    C. because it has a long, pointed beak.

Trees

There are many kinds of trees. Some trees grow fruit.
Other trees grow nuts. Some trees have flowers on them.
All trees need sun and rain to grow.

Directions: Match words to pictures. Draw lines.

1. All trees need this to grow.

A.

2. Some trees grow fruit.

B.

3. Some trees have flowers.

C.

4. Some trees grow nuts.

D.

Special Clothes

Many people wear special clothes, called **uniforms**, for their jobs. Uniforms help other people to know a person's job right away. Doctors, nurses, fire fighters, and other helpers wear uniforms.

Directions: Draw a line to show which person can help you.

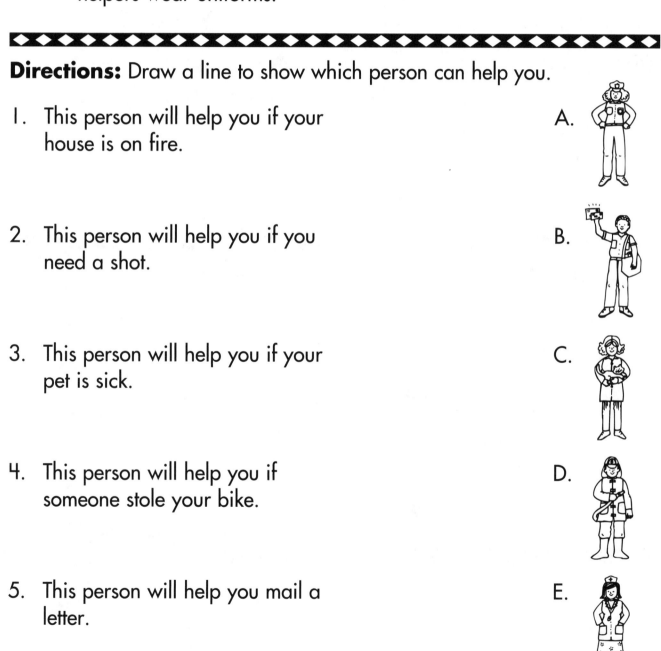

1. This person will help you if your house is on fire.

   A.

2. This person will help you if you need a shot.

   B.

3. This person will help you if your pet is sick.

   C.

4. This person will help you if someone stole your bike.

   D.

5. This person will help you mail a letter.

   E.

Deserts

A desert is very dry land. This land gets little rain. The air is hot during the day. At night, the desert air becomes very cool. The wind blows the sand into small hills called **sand dunes**. Some deserts have dirt instead of sand. Only a few kinds of plants and animals can live in such a hot, dry place.

Directions: Circle **Yes** or **No**. Show what might happen in a desert.

1. There is a rain storm every night in the desert.

    Yes   **No**

2. The wind makes new sand dunes in the desert.

    Yes   **No**

3. The desert gets cool during the day.

    Yes   **No**

4. Many trees grow in the desert.

    Yes   **No**

5. A camel can walk across the desert.

    Yes   **No**

6. A desert can have dirt instead of sand.

    Yes   **No**

Going to the Doctor

Jason woke up one morning, and his head hurt. His mother said, "You feel hot. You better stay home from school."

Jason rested all day. He still did not feel good. His mother said, "You need to go see the doctor."

The doctor took Jason's temperature. He looked in Jason's throat and his ears. Then he said, "Jason, you need to do two things to get well."

Directions: Circle the two things that Jason's doctor probably told him to do.

Name_____ Date_____

Time for a Picnic

Mr. Watson's class is planning a picnic. Everyone is going to bring something to eat or drink.

"I will get lemons and make something cold to drink," said Ali.

"I will get vegetables to make something crunchy to eat," said Celia.

"I will bring a cold and sweet dessert," said Anna.

"I will bring something sweet that my mom will bake," said Sam.

Directions: What will each student bring to the picnic? Draw a line.

1. Celia

2. Anna

3. Sam

4. Ali

A.

B.

C.

D.

What's the Weather?

Every day Mr. Brown's class reads a weather report from their pen pals on the Internet. This is today's report.

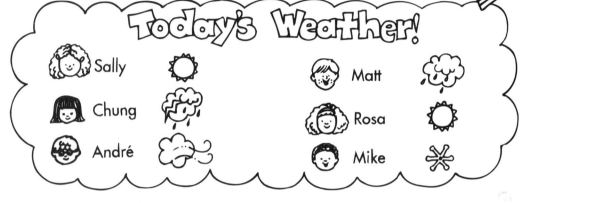

Directions: Look at the report to help you circle the right answers.

1. Who has sunny weather today?

   A. Sally and Matt

   B. Chung and Rosa

   C. Sally and Rosa

   D. André and Mike

2. Who has snow today?

   A. Mike

   B. Matt

   C. Rosa

   D. Chung

3. Who has rain today?

   A. Sally and Chung

   B. Mike and Chung

   C. Matt and Chung

   D. André and Chung

4. Who could fly a kite today?

   A. André

   B. Matt

   C. Mike

   D. Chung

What Happens Next?

One morning, Chris could not find his homework. He looked in his room. He looked in the kitchen. Then he looked at his dog, Ruff. Ruff liked to hide things in his dog bed.

Li picks strawberries. He washes them well. He puts them in a bowl. He gets a spoon out of a drawer.

Directions: Read each story. Then answer the question.

1. Where did Chris find his homework?

   A. in his room

   B. in Ruff's bed

   C. in the kitchen

2. What does Li do next?

   A. washes the strawberries

   B. goes outside

   C. eats the strawberries

Happy Birthday!

Gina helped plan her brother's birthday party. She helped to shop for the party. She set the table. Here is a picture of the table right before the party.

Directions: Look at the picture. Then answer the questions.

1. What do you think the guests will be wearing?

   A. snow boots

   B. party hats

   C. mittens

   D. masks

2. What is one snack the guests will be eating?

   A. pasta

   B. soda pop

   C. popcorn

   D. turkey

3. How old do you think Gina's brother is?

   A. two

   B. four

   C. five

   D. seven

4. What is one thing that Gina bought for the party?

   A. a drum

   B. a grill

   C. teddy bears

   D. a tablecloth

Chick and Duck

Chick thought that Duck was mad at him. Duck was sitting all by himself. Chick asked Duck what was wrong. He gave Duck treats and toys. At last, Duck said, "I am not mad. I just want to be alone for a while. We are still best friends."

Directions: Circle the right answer.

1. Why did Chick think that Duck was mad?

   A. because Duck said he was mad

   B. because Duck was sitting by himself

   C. because Duck did not want the treats or toys

2. Why did Duck want to sit by himself?

   A. because he was mad

   B. because he did not like Chick

   C. because he wanted to be alone for a while

3. Which picture shows a real bird?

   A.

   B.

   C.

No More Trash!

Polly Packrat lived in the Green Woods. She liked to collect junk. She had rocks and cans. She had string, nuts, leaves, and sticks. She piled them all on her floor.

Mother Packrat looked at the mess. She said, "No more trash! Clean up this room!"

Polly filled up her wagon. She walked to the dump. She was sad. Then she saw a blue stone on the ground. It had rolled off the wagon. The pretty stone cheered Polly up.

Directions: Write **T** for true or **F** for false.

1. _____ Real packrats can talk.

2. _____ Real animals have wagons.

3. _____ Polly Packrat is not like a real animal.

4. _____ Polly and her mother are characters in a story.

Name_____ Date _____

Clowns

Clowns are fun to watch. They are actors who like to make you laugh. Clowns wear make-up and wigs to look funny. They wear funny costumes and big shoes. Sometimes a clown will have a big, red rubber nose over his real nose. Clowns learn how to do tricks. You can see clowns in parades and at the circus.

Directions: Circle the right answer.

1. Which sentence is true?

   A. Clowns are not real people.

   B. You can see clowns every day in your neighborhood.

   C. Clowns are actors dressed in special clothes and make-up.

   D. Clowns are real people who are strange.

2. Which things do clowns not wear?

   A. red rubber noses

   B. big shoes

   C. funny costumes

   D. police uniforms

3. Why do clowns do tricks?

   A. to cheat people

   B. to make people laugh

   C. to make people cry

   D. to learn things

4. Write one place you have seen a clown.

   _____

   _ _ _ _ _ _ _ _ _ _ _ _ _

   _____

   _ _ _ _ _ _ _ _ _ _ _ _ _

   _____

◆◆◆◆◆◆◆◆◆◆◆◆◆◆◆◆◆◆◆◆◆◆◆◆◆◆◆◆◆◆

If I Had Wings

If I had wings,
I would fly very high.
I would see everything
If I could fly!
I would fly to school,
And eat clouds for ice cream,
But I only fly
At night, in my dreams.

◆◆◆◆◆◆◆◆◆◆◆◆◆◆◆◆◆◆◆◆◆◆◆◆◆◆◆◆◆◆

Directions: Answer the questions.

1. Can the person in the poem really fly?

   Yes   **No**

   How do you know? _____

   – – – – – – – – – – – –
   _____
   _____
   – – – – – – – – – – – –
   _____
   _____
   – – – – – – – – – – – –
   _____
   _____
   – – – – – – – – – – – –
   _____

2. If the person in the poem could fly, what would she do?

   A. fly at night

   B. fly to school

   C. fly to the moon

   D. fly to a party

3. If you could fly, where would you go? _____

   – – – – – – – – – – – –
   _____
   _____
   – – – – – – – – – – – –
   _____

Walking to Mars

Michelle learned all about the stars and planets.
She read about the planet Mars. Mars was
her favorite planet. Michelle wanted to see
Mars herself. She pulled stars from the sky.
She made stairs from the stars.
Then Michelle walked up the
starry staircase to Mars.

Directions: Circle the right answer.

1. In the story, how did Michelle go to Mars?

   A. She flew to Mars in an airplane.

   B. She went to Mars in a rocket.

   C. She built stairs to Mars and walked.

2. How did Michelle build a staircase?

   A. out of stars

   B. out of clouds

   C. out of planets

3. Which helped you know that this story is not about a real event?

   A. Michelle learned about the stars.

   B. Michelle pulled stars from the sky.

   C. Michelle read about the planet Mars.

   D. Michelle's favorite planet was Mars.

4. Write on the line. What is your favorite planet?

   _____

   _ _ _ _ _ _ _ _ _ _ _ _ _ _

   _____

The Moon

Dear Chung,

    Do you ever look at the moon at night? We learned about the moon at school today. It travels around Earth. It gets its light from the sun. Astronauts have gone to the moon in a spaceship. They have walked on the moon. They even brought back moon rocks to study. Would you like to walk on the moon some day? I would!

Your friend,

Tio

Directions: Circle **Yes** or **No** to answer each question.

1. Have astronauts really walked on the moon?

    Yes   **No**

2. Did astronauts fly to the moon in a spaceship?

    Yes   **No**

3. Can you drive a car to the moon?

    Yes   **No**

4. Does this picture show a real walk on the moon?

    Yes   **No**

Horseback Riding

Have you ever been horseback riding? Many people ride today because they think it is fun. People like to train horses to race or to jump. Long ago, horses were not kept as pets. People had to ride horses to go from one place to another. They also rode horses to hunt for food. Horses pulled wagons and helped to plow fields.

Directions: Write **F** for fact or **O** for opinion.

1. _____ Horseback riding is the best sport.

2. _____ Long ago, people needed horses to hunt for food.

3. _____ Today, people like to train horses to race or jump.

4. _____ Horses are the smartest animals on Earth.

Police

Dear Angela,

    Today, a police officer came to our class. I thought she was the best speaker we have ever had! She talked about her job. She said that the police help keep people safe. They make sure people obey laws. Some police officers ride in cars. Others ride bikes. Some ride motorcycles. Some police even fly helicopters! I think that would be a great job. Don't you?

                                        Yours truly,

                                        Maria

Directions: Circle the right answer. Write an answer for question 3.

1. Which of these is a fact?

    A. Police officers are great speakers in class.

    B. Some police officers ride in cars.

    C. Flying a police helicopter would be a great job.

2. Which of these is an opinion?

    A. The police help keep people safe.

    B. Some police fly in helicopters.

    C. Flying a police helicopter would be a great job.

3. Would you like to be a police officer?

    _____

    - - - - - - - - - - - -

    _____

◆◆◆

Pilots

A pilot is a person who flies an airplane. Pilots go to special schools to learn how to fly planes. Some pilots fly planes for fun. Other pilots fly planes as their job. Pilots have to learn how to fly in all kinds of weather. They have to work with people on the ground to land planes safely. Being a pilot is an important job.

◆◆◆

Directions: Connect the two parts of the fact sentences together. Draw lines.

1. Pilots go to special schools   A. for fun.

2. Some pilots fly planes   B. of weather.

3. Pilots have to fly in all kinds   C. flies an airplane.

4. A pilot is a person who   D. to learn how to fly planes.

---

5. Circle the fact.

   A. Pilots must have a lot of fun flying planes.

   B. It must be scary to fly in a storm.

   C. Some pilots fly planes as their job.

   D. All pilots are very brave.

Fire Fighters

A fire fighter's job is to put out fires. This can be a dangerous job. Sometimes fire fighters have to go into burning houses. Sometimes they have to get people out safely. Whenever the bell rings, the fire fighters rush to their truck. They wear special boots, hats, and coats to help keep them safe from the fire.

Directions: Write **F** for fact or **O** for opinion.

1. _____ A fire fighter's job is to put out fires.

2. _____ A fire fighter's job is scary.

3. _____ Fire fighters wear special clothes to help keep them safe.

4. _____ I would not want to be a fire fighter.

5. _____ Fire fighters rush to their truck when the bell rings.

6. _____ Fire fighters drive a special truck.

The Storm

We looked out the window. A tornado was headed right to our house! We ran into the bathroom and closed the door. All three of us got into the bathtub. I could hear a loud roar. It sounded like a train. My heart was pounding.

Later, I found out that summer is the time when most tornadoes happen. These storms can knock down houses and other buildings. Sometimes, the tornado can pick up a car or a tree right off the ground. We were lucky because our house was not hurt. We were not hurt, either!

Directions: Connect the two parts of the fact sentences. Draw lines.

1. Tornados often happen   A. houses and other buildings.

2. A tornado can knock down   B. like a train.

3. A tornado makes a loud roar   C. in the summer.

4. A tornado can pick up   D. cars or trees.

Sharla's Baby Brother

My new baby brother, Ty, is the loudest baby in the world. It seems like he never stops crying. He cries all day long. He cries just as I am falling asleep at night. Mom has to guess what Ty wants, because he can't tell us.

Sometimes Ty stops crying. Then he is the cutest baby in the world! He has black hair and dark brown eyes. He likes to wave his hands in the air. He has a great smile.

Directions: Circle **F** for fact or **O** for opinion.

1. **F** **O** Ty is the loudest baby in the world.

2. **F** **O** Ty is the cutest baby in the world.

3. **F** **O** Ty has black hair and dark brown eyes.

4. **F** **O** Ty likes to wave his hands in the air.

5. **F** **O** Ty can't tell his family what he wants.

6. **F** **O** Ty shouldn't cry so much.

The Post Office

The post office is the place that takes care of the mail. You can go there to mail your letters and packages. You pay to have your mail sent to other people. They pay to send mail to you. Some mail is sent far away. Mail is sent in many different ways. It can be sent on planes or trains.

Directions: Circle the right answer.

1. Which thing can you buy at the post office?

A.

B.

C.

2. What is one way that mail is sent?

A.

B.

C.

3. Which is something that you can mail?

A.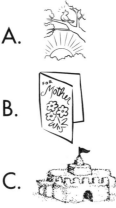

B.

C.

4. What do you give the post office to send your mail?

A.

B.

C.

New Gardens

Marsha and Tim plant gardens. They buy seeds.

Here are Marsha's seeds.

Here are Tim's seeds.

Directions: Circle the right answer.

1. Aunt Susie wants to plant beans. Where will she plant them?

    A. Marsha's garden

    B. Tim's garden

2. Where will Marsha put what she grows?

    A. in a tire

    B. in a vase

    C. in soup

3. What will Tim be able to make from his garden?

    A. bread

    B. a book

    C. a salad

4. Circle the garden tools.

    A.

    B. (saw)

    C.

    D.

Riddle Time

When you read a riddle, you are playing a game to answer it. The riddle gives you clues. From the clues, you can guess what the riddle is about.

Directions: Read each food riddle. Then match it to the right picture.

1. I am orange and round. You can give me a grin.

    A.

2. I am sweet, but don't slip on my peel!

    B.

3. I am red and crunchy. Give me to your teacher.

    C.

4. Dig me up from the ground. You can make fries from me!

    D.

Glassfish

Glassfish are small fish. Most live in the ocean, but some live in fresh water in India. You can see through a glassfish's skin. You can even see its bones! Some people have glassfish for pets. They are hard to raise in a tank. They live better in the sea.

Directions: Circle the right answer.

1. How do you think the glassfish got its name?

   A. because it is full of water

   B. because it is made from glass

   C. because you can see through its skin

2. Which one is a glassfish?

   A.

   B.

   C.

3. Why do you think glassfish live better in the sea?

   A. because they are made of glass

   B. because they want to live in tanks

   C. because the sea is their home

4. What kind of fish is a glassfish?

   A. large

   B. small

   C. dark-colored

Name_____ Date _____

The Stagecoach

People have not always had cars. Long ago, a stagecoach was the best way to go from one town to another. This big coach needed four or six horses to pull it. The stagecoach carried people. It also took mail from one place to another. Stagecoach trips could take days. The ride was bumpy and hard. But it was better than other ways of travel.

Directions: Circle the right answer.

1. Why did people use stagecoaches?

   A. because they liked horses

   B. because they liked bumpy trips

   C. because there were no cars

2. Why do you think riding in a stagecoach was bumpy and hard?

   A. because the roads were not good

   B. because the wheels were the wrong size

   C. because the horses moved too fast

3. What is one reason that a stagecoach would be better than riding a horse?

   A. It would protect you from rain or snow.

   B. Riding a horse would be slower.

   C. You could not ride a horse on bumpy roads.

20 MILES TO

Astronauts

An astronaut is a person who travels in space. Only a few people can become astronauts. After a person is picked, he or she has to go to a special school. Astronauts can spend years learning everything they need to know for space travel. They must know all about their spaceships. They must be smart. They must be very healthy. Astronauts work hard to get ready for their jobs.

1. Why does an astronaut have to go to a special school?

   A. because space travel is not taught in other schools

   B. because traveling in space is fun

   C. because astronauts must be healthy

2. Why do you think that an astronaut needs to be smart?

   A. to learn about the stars

   B. to help out if something goes wrong

   C. to be able to exercise

3. Which of these people do you think would make the best astronaut?

   A. a gardener

   B. a skater

   C. a scientist

Eli Elephant

Eli Elephant loves to garden. He waters the plants with his trunk. He eats the vegetables as soon as they are ripe. Eli is gray. He has a long trunk. He wears a hat to keep safe from the hot sun. He loves to wear old, soft overalls.

Directions: Circle **Yes** or **No** to answer each question.

1. Eli loves to garden.

    Yes   **No**

2. Eli likes brand-new overalls.

    Yes   **No**

3. Eli wears a hat to keep safe from the sun.

    Yes   **No**

4. Eli sells his vegetables at the market.

    Yes   **No**

5. Eli waters his plants with a garden hose.

    Yes   **No**

Name _____ Date _____

The Farmer

Mack is a farmer. He has an important job. He grows food that we eat. Mack grows wheat and oats. He also takes care of the animals on his farm. Mack works hard. He gets up early every day. He works until it is dark. He loves helping the young plants grow. He smiles as he works. In the fall, he harvests his crops. The wheat is made into bread. The oats are made into cereal.

Directions: Circle the right answer.

1. How do you know that Mack works hard?

   A. He grows wheat and oats.

   B. He gets up early and works late.

   C. He has an important job.

2. How do you know that Mack likes being a farmer?

   A. He smiles as he works.

   B. He harvests his crops.

   C. He grows oats for cereal.

3. What happens to the wheat that Mack grows?

   A. It is made into cereal.

   B. It is made into dinners.

   C. It is made into bread.

4. Why is Mack's job important?

   A. Farmers smile as they work.

   B. Farmers grow the food we eat.

   C. Farmers work hard.

Up and Away

I fasten my belt and close my eyes.
The next time I look, we're up in the skies!
Mom reads her book, but I look outside.
I feel like a bird on this airplane ride.
Blue sky above and white clouds below.
I look out the window and watch the show!

Directions: Circle the right answer.

1. How is this child traveling?

   A.

   B.

   C.

2. What does the child do first?

   A.

   B.

   C.

3. What does the child see below?

   A.

   B.

   C.

4. Where must the child be sitting?

   A.

   B.

   C.

Name _____ Date _____

At the Airport

An airport is a busy place. It is where planes take off and land on runways. People line up to buy tickets for the planes. Their bags are driven to the plane in open trucks. The airport has places where you can eat and buy gifts. You can buy a book to read on your flight. There are also places with big windows where you can watch the planes land.

Directions: Match the words to the pictures that show things in the airport.

1. A plane takes off on the runway.

A.

2. People buy tickets for the plane.

B.

3. People can eat at the airport.

C.

TICKETS

4. Bags are taken to the plane in open trucks.

D.

My Favorite Place

My favorite place is a wonderful store.
If you would like, I'll tell you more.
There are cases of dolls,
Tiny beds, little chairs.
There are shelves full of animals—
Stuffed mice and stuffed bears!

Directions: Write **T** for true or **F** for false.

1. _____ This poem is about a clothing store.

2. _____ The bears are on shelves.

3. _____ The tiny beds and little chairs are for dolls.

4. _____ Stuffed animals are sold in this store.

5. _____ The poem says that the store sells toy trains.

6. _____ The mice in the poem are real.

Name _____ Date _____

Icebergs

There are big sheets of ice on the South Pole and near the North Pole. Sometimes pieces break off from these sheets. The pieces float out in the ocean. They are called **icebergs**.

If you were crossing the ocean, you might see an iceberg. Icebergs can be big. Some are as big as mountains. But often, only a tip of the iceberg can be seen above the water. Most of the iceberg is below water. As icebergs float into warmer water, they melt and become part of the ocean's water.

Directions: Circle the right answer.

1. If you were on an iceberg, it would be—

   A. cold and slippery.

   B. warm and cozy.

   C. dry and hot.

2. Icebergs can be—

   A. as big as mountains.

   B. too cold to melt.

   C. as big as an ocean.

3. Icebergs may be hard to see because—

   A. they are as big as mountains.

   B. they are floating away.

   C. only a tip shows above the water.

4. What happens to an iceberg?

   A. It becomes part of the North Pole again.

   B. It turns into a mountain.

   C. It melts and becomes part of the ocean's water.

A Fall Day

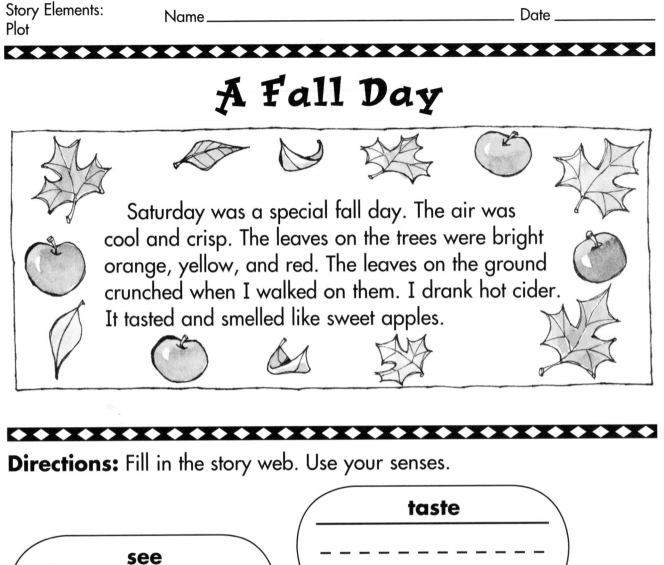

Saturday was a special fall day. The air was cool and crisp. The leaves on the trees were bright orange, yellow, and red. The leaves on the ground crunched when I walked on them. I drank hot cider. It tasted and smelled like sweet apples.

Directions: Fill in the story web. Use your senses.

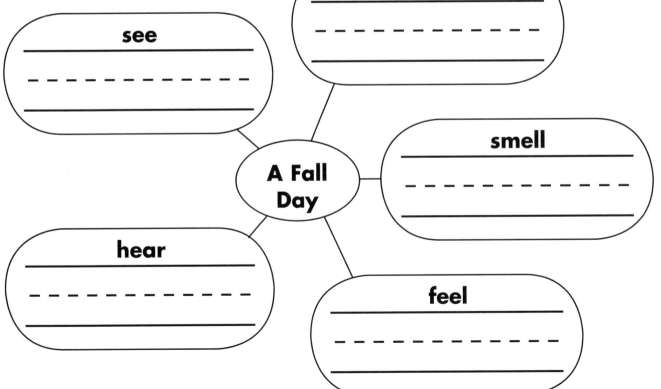

taste
_____
- - - - - - - - -
_____

see
_____
- - - - - - - - -
_____

smell
_____
- - - - - - - - -
_____

A Fall Day

hear
_____
- - - - - - - - -
_____

feel
_____
- - - - - - - - -
_____

A Trip to the Farm

I am so excited! Today, I get to visit Aunt Jenna.

Aunt Jenna has a farm. When I visit her, I get to pet all the animals. Aunt Jenna lets me bake cookies. We pick vegetables from her garden. We plant flowers.

I am packing my suitcase. It will be a great trip!

Directions: Match the words with the pictures. Draw a line.

1. pet the animals

A.

2. bake cookies

B.

3. pick vegetables

C.

4. plant flowers

D.

Sharing

Wendy was Tanya's baby sister. Wendy wanted to do everything that Tanya did. Tanya was going to eat the last piece of cake. But there was a problem. Wendy wanted to eat a piece, too. Tanya had an idea. She cut the piece of cake in half. The two sisters ate their snack together.

Directions: Circle the right answer.

1. Which one is Tanya?

   A.

   B.

   C.

2. What did Wendy want to eat?

   A.

   B.

   C.

3. Who is Wendy?

   A. She is Tanya's cousin.

   B. She is Tanya's cat.

   C. She is Tanya's sister.

4. How did Tanya fix her problem?

   A. She shared the cake.

   B. She put Wendy to bed.

   C. She threw away the cake.

A Strange Meeting

Terry was sitting by the river. He felt a bump on the back of his shell. An owl had landed on him!

"Excuse me," said Terry. "Would you please move?"

"Oh!" said Olive Owl. "I am so sorry. I thought you were a rock."

Olive flew to a tree. Terry pulled his head inside his shell and went to sleep.

Directions: Circle **Yes** or **No** to answer each question.

1. Terry is a turtle.

   Yes   **No**

2. Terry felt a seagull land on his shell.

   Yes   **No**

3. Olive thought that Terry was a rock.

   Yes   **No**

4. At the end of the story, Terry goes for a swim.

   Yes   **No**

A Day Off

Jean's family does something
special on Labor Day. They all go
to a hospital in their town. Everyone
in her family is given a job to do.
Jean gets to bring books to the
patients, the people in the hospital
rooms. Because Jean's family works,
some of the hospital workers can have the day off. After
the family is done working, they have a picnic in the park.

1. Why does Jean's family go to
   the hospital on Labor Day?

   A. because they are hurt

   B. because they are ill

   C. because they are helping

2. What does Jean do on Labor
   Day?

   A. She takes books to patients.

   B. She watches fireworks.

   C. She cooks for the patients.

3. Why does Jean's family work
   at the hospital?

   A. They think it is fun.

   B. They let hospital workers
      have a day off.

   C. They like to take books to
      people.

4. What does Jean's family do at
   the end of the day?

   A. They go swimming.

   B. They go riding.

   C. They have a picnic.

At the Beach

Jaleel and his family went to the beach. Dad went swimming. Mom read a book.

Jaleel and his brother wanted to build a sand castle. They used pails to make part of the castle. They filled the pails with wet sand. Then they turned them upside down to make towers. They used shells to make the castle look nice.

At the end of the day, the tide came in. The waves washed over the castle. It turned back into sand on the beach.

Directions: Match the parts of the sentences to show what happened. Draw lines.

1. Jaleel and his family

A. build a sand castle.

2. Jaleel and his brother wanted to

B. to make towers for the castle.

3. The two brothers used pails

C. went to the beach.

4. Jaleel and his brother used shells

D. washed over the castle.

E. to make the castle look nice.

5. At the end of the day, the waves

Riding Bikes

Carol and Ramon wanted to ride bikes together. They were going to ride to the playground. But when Carol went to get her bike, she had a problem. Her bike had a flat tire.

"Don't worry," said Ramon. "Walk your bike to my house. My mom can fix the tire for you."

Directions: Circle the right answer.

1. Which picture shows what was wrong with Carol's bike?

    A.

    B.

    C.

2. Find the picture that shows where Carol and Ramon wanted to go.

    A.

    B.

    C.

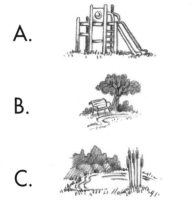

3. How was Carol's problem solved?

    A. Ramon's mom would fix the tire.

    B. Ramon fixed the tire.

    C. Carol's mom fixed the tire.

4. What probably happens after the bike is fixed?

    A. Carol and Ramon eat a snack.

    B. Carol and Ramon go to the playground.

    C. Carol goes back to her house.

Learning About Bees

Dear Grandma,

    This week in school we learned about bees. Did you know that bees work together and help each other? In their home, called a **hive**, there are three kinds of bees. One kind are the worker bees. The worker bees all have jobs. They clean the hive. They take care of the baby bees. Some of them fan their wings to keep the hive cool! Worker bees are also the ones you see flying in the garden. They get nectar from the flowers. The **nectar** is turned into honey back at the hive.

Love,

Corey

Directions: Write in the web. What fits on the blank line?

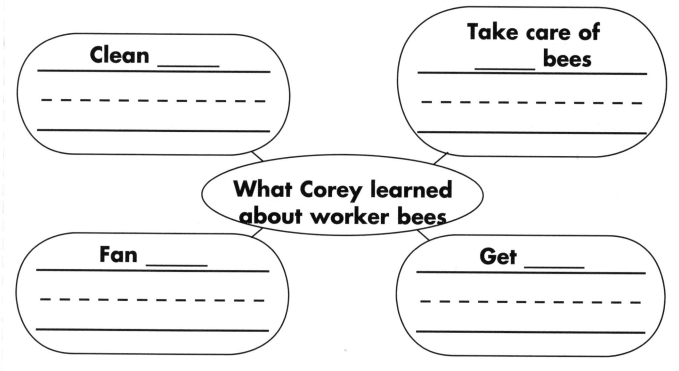

Clean _____

Take care of _____ bees

Fan _____

What Corey learned about worker bees

Get _____

The Lost Pet

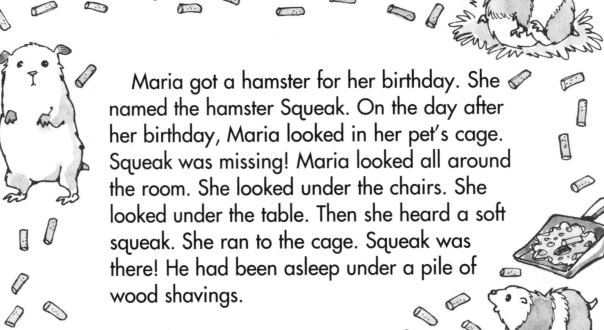

Maria got a hamster for her birthday. She named the hamster Squeak. On the day after her birthday, Maria looked in her pet's cage. Squeak was missing! Maria looked all around the room. She looked under the chairs. She looked under the table. Then she heard a soft squeak. She ran to the cage. Squeak was there! He had been asleep under a pile of wood shavings.

Directions: Circle **T** for true or **F** for false.

1. The first place Maria looked was in Squeak's cage.

   T   **F**

2. Next, Maria looked under the table.

   T   **F**

3. Maria ran upstairs to look for Squeak.

   T   **F**

4. It turned out that Squeak was not really lost.

   T   **F**

Animal Friends

Big Bear, Little Bear, Silve[r]
All live with me under one
They are my friends. They
    sleep on my bed.
They never need
    walking or need to
    be fed.
I tell them my secrets,
    and they never speak.
They don't make a sound,
    not even a squeak.

Directions: Circle the right answer.

1. What is this poem about?

    A. animals who live in the woods

    B. toy animals on a girl's bed

    C. pets who live in a kennel

2. What kind of animal do you think Woof is?

    A. a real dog

    B. a toy dog

    C. a toy horse

3. What is the setting for the animals?

    A. in a kitchen

    B. in a garage

    C. in a bedroom

4. How are these animals different from real pets?

    A. They are friends.

    B. They sleep on a bed.

    C. They never need to be fed.

Name_____ Date _____

Lunch Time

Juan was hungry. He wanted to eat lunch. Here's what he did.
First, Juan got out two slices of bread.
Second, he opened a jar of peanut butter and a jar of jelly.
Then, Juan spread peanut butter on one piece of bread.
Next, he spread jelly on the other piece of bread.
Last, he put the two slices of bread together.

Directions: Circle the right answer.

1. What did Juan do first?

   A. spread peanut butter on bread

   B. got out two slices of bread

   C. spread jelly on bread

2. What did Juan do after he had spread peanut butter and jelly on the bread?

   A. He opened a jar of jelly.

   B. He put the two slices of bread together.

   C. He ate the two slices of bread.

3. Why did Juan get out the bread, jelly, and peanut butter?

   A. because he liked bread

   B. because he wanted to play

   C. because he was hungry

4. What did Juan make?

   A. a sandwich

   B. a cookie

   C. a sundae

Trisha's Pet

Cat
Shy, green-eyed
Purring, yawning, sleeping
Tiger

Directions: Circle the right answer.

1. Who is Tiger?

   A. a jungle animal

   B. Trisha's cat

   C. a pet dog

2. What kind of cat is Tiger?

   A. shy and friendly

   B. mean and hissing

   C. brave and noisy

3. Which of these probably tells what Tiger looks like?

   A. a black cat with yellow eyes

   B. a white cat with blue eyes

   C. a striped cat with green eyes

4. What else can you tell about Tiger from the poem?

   A. He likes to take naps.

   B. He likes to hunt outside.

   C. He likes to eat fish.

A News Story

Today, a young girl told the police that her sheep were lost. She did not know where to find them. The police officer told the girl to leave the sheep alone. He was sure that the sheep would come home by themselves.

Directions: Circle the right answer.

1. Who is the young girl in the story?

   A. Little Miss Muffet

   B. Goldilocks

   C. Little Bo-Peep

2. What is the girl's problem?

   A. She can't find her house.

   B. She can't find her sheep.

   C. She can't find her dog.

3. What did the police officer tell the girl?

   A. to go looking for the sheep

   B. to ask people if they had seen the sheep

   C. to leave the sheep alone

4. How do you think this story will end?

   A. The sheep will come home.

   B. The sheep will stay lost.

   C. She will find the sheep herself.

Ice Cream .... **Page 4**
1. 2, 3, 1
2. hot
3. Answers will vary.

The Bus .... **Page 5**
1. B
2. C
3. A

Trains .... **Page 6**
1. A
2. C
3. B
4. tracks

Days .... **Page 7**
1. B
2. C
3. A
4. Answers will vary.

The Baseball Game .... **Page 8**
1. C
2. B
3. C
4. Answers will vary.

The Spider .... **Page 9**
1. A
2. B
3. Yes
4. Yes
5. No

Penny .... **Page 10**
1. C
2. B
3. C
4. Answers will vary.

A Falling Star .... **Page 11**
1. 3, 1, 2
2. C
3. B

My Feelings .... **Page 12**
1. B
2. D
3. A
4. C
5. happy
6. sad
7. angry
8. surprised

Names .... **Page 13**
People Names: Mary, Jesse
Pet Names: Fluffy, Goldie
Town Names: Smithville, Portland

School .... **Page 14**
1. B
2. D
3. A
4. C
5. Answers will vary.
6. Answers will vary.

Fruits and Vegetables .... **Page 15**
1. V
2. V
3. F
4. V
5. F
6. Banana should be circled.

Baby Animals .... **Page 16**
1. B
2. C
3. D
4. A

All the Animals .... **Page 17**
1. M
2. R
3. B
4. M
5. B
6. M

Months of the Year .... **Page 18**
Chart should be filled in appropriately.

Shopping .... **Page 19**
1. 3
2. 5
3. 4
4. 2
5. 1
6. 6

Kites .... **Page 20**
1. C
2. B
3. C
4. Answers will vary.

Way Out West .... **Page 21**
1. A
2. C
3. D
4. Cowboy hat should be circled.

Letters .... **Page 22**
1. T
2. F
3. T
4. T
5. Answers will vary.
6. Answers will vary.

Answer Key

Money .... **Page 23**
1. A
2. B
3. B
4. C

Snakes .... **Page 24**
1. T
2. T
3. F
4. F
5. F

Sun Bears .... **Page 25**
1. sun
2. orange
3. trees
4. day
5. nests
6. night

Hobbies .... **Page 26**
1. hobbies
2. Answers will vary.
3. Answers will vary.
4. likes
5. Answers will vary.

Pets .... **Page 27**
1. Nell
2. Ang
3. Marla
4. Rob
5. B

Birds .... **Page 28**
1. B
2. C
3. D
4. E
5. A

The New Puppy .... **Page 29**
What Ling Looks Like: tan, soft fur, black nose
What Ling Needs: special food, warm bed, rest

Stars .... **Page 30**
1. B
2. B
3. T
4. T
5. T
6. F

Starfish .... **Page 31**
1. D
2. A
3. B
4. C

A Letter to Juan .... **Page 32**
1. B
2. C
3. C
4. B

At the Mall .... **Page 33**
fan: Dad, truck: John, scarf: Lisa, vase: Mom

Fall .... **Page 34**
1. cool
2. food
3. crops
4. yards

Maggie's Report .... **Page 35**
Sentences 2 and 5 should be crossed out.

Clouds .... **Page 36**
1. B
2. C
3. C
4. A

Weather .... **Page 37**
1. A
2. B
3. weather
4. Plants

Seals .... **Page 38**
1. Yes
2. No
3. Yes
4. No

A Rabbit Poem .... **Page 39**
1. Answers will vary. Sentence should indicate that the poem tells what rabbits look like and what they like to eat.
2. Answers will vary. Sentences should indicate that rabbits are small, have a fluffy tail, and have long ears.

The Earth .... **Page 40**
1. C
2. A
3. D
4. A

Football .... **Page 41**
1. Answers will vary. Sentence should indicate that the story tells about the sport of football and how it is played.
2. It takes the whole team to win a football game.

Nelly Bly .... **Page 42**
1. B
2. A
3. B

Big Dogs, Little Dogs .... **Page 43**
Little Dogs: can sit on your lap, can be noisy, can live indoors
Big Dogs: may live outside, need more food and space, can guard a house
Both Dogs: are great pets, can be good friends

◆◇◆◇◆◇◆◇◆◇◆◇◆◇◆◇◆◇◆◇◆◇◆◇◆◇◆◇◆◇◆◇◆◇◆◇◆

Winter Fun.. **Page 44**

1. B
2. C
3. B
4. Hat should be drawn and colored in picture.

Snow... **Page 45**

1. T
2. F
3. F
4. T
5. T
6. F

Parks.. **Page 46**

1. D
2. B
3. A
4. C
5. Answers will vary.

Bike Safety .... **Page 47**

1. B
2. C
3. D
4. A

Foxes.. **Page 48**

1. C
2. B
3. D
4. A

The Days Grow Short............................. **Page 49**

1. A
2. C
3. B
4. D

All Kinds of Boats .... **Page 50**

1. sailboat
2. fireboat
3. rowboat
4. houseboat
5. tugboat

The Rodeo.. **Page 51**

1. D
2. C
3. B
4. A

Too Hot! Too Cold! .... **Page 52**

1. too cold
2. too hot
3. too hot
4. too cold
5. too hot
6. too cold

Dinosaurs .... **Page 53**

All dinosaurs: very big animals
Dinosaurs ate: meat, plants
Dinosaurs traveled by: flying

Elephants and Giraffes............................. **Page 54**

1. F
2. T
3. F
4. T
5. T
6. F

Time .... **Page 55**

1. A
2. D
3. A
4. C

Penguins and Robins .... **Page 56**

1. A
2. B
3. A
4. B

Wolves .... **Page 57**

1. T
2. T
3. F
4. F
5. T

Map Facts .... **Page 58**

1. A
2. A
3. B
4. A
5. B

Zoo Riddles.. **Page 59**

1. zebra
2. lion
3. seal
4. giraffe

The Sun... **Page 60**

1. sun
2. gives
3. warm
4. Sun should be drawn and colored yellow in picture.

Traffic Signs .... **Page 61**

1. Stop
2. Go
3. Stop
4. Go

Who Is First?.. **Page 62**

Writing lines should be filled in in this order: Wednesday, Tuesday, Thursday, Monday, Friday

Wonderful Wheels .... **Page 63**

No bikes, no wagons, no trucks, no trains (or no planes)

Answer Key

◆◆◆◆◆◆◆◆◆◆◆◆◆◆◆◆◆◆◆◆◆◆◆◆◆◆◆◆◆◆◆◆◆◆◆◆◆◆

Pilots .... **Page 86**
1. D
2. A
3. B
4. C
5. C

Fire Fighters .... **Page 87**
1. F
2. O
3. F
4. O
5. F
6. F

A Pet Story .... **Page 88**
1. D
2. B
3. Answers will vary.
4. Answers will vary.

Figs .... **Page 89**
1. blue
2. red
3. red
4. blue
5. red
6. blue

The Storm .... **Page 90**
1. C
2. A
3. B
4. D

Sharla's Baby Brother .... **Page 91**
1. O
2. O
3. F
4. F
5. F
6. O

The Post Office .... **Page 92**
1. A
2. C
3. B
4. C

New Gardens .... **Page 93**
1. B
2. B
3. C
4. A and D should be circled.

Thank-you Letters .... **Page 94**
1. C
2. A
3. B

A Party .... **Page 95**
1. C
2. B
3. C
4. Answers will vary.

Riddle Time .... **Page 96**
1. C
2. D
3. A
4. B

Glassfish .... **Page 97**
1. C
2. A
3. C
4. B

The Stagecoach .... **Page 98**
1. C
2. A
3. A

Astronauts .... **Page 99**
1. A
2. B
3. C

Dolly .... **Page 100**
1. C
2. D
3. A
4. E
5. B

The Basketball Player .... **Page 101**

Anna's Height: Tall
Anna's Hair Color: Black
Anna's Sport: Basketball
How Anna Feels: Happy, Proud

Eli Elephant .... **Page 102**
1. Yes
2. No
3. Yes
4. No
5. No

The Farmer .... **Page 103**
1. B
2. A
3. C
4. B

Up and Away .... **Page 104**
1. C
2. A
3. B
4. B

Answer Key

◆◆◆◆◆◆◆◆◆◆◆◆◆◆◆◆◆◆◆◆◆◆◆◆◆◆◆◆◆◆◆◆◆◆◆

At the Airport .... Page 105

1. D
2. C
3. A
4. B

The Taxi Ride .... Page 106

1. No
2. Yes
3. Yes
4. No
5. Yes

Camping Trip .... Page 107

1. C
2. B
3. C
4. A

My Favorite Place .... Page 108

1. F
2. T
3. T
4. T
5. F
6. F

Icebergs .... Page 109

1. A
2. A
3. C
4. C

A Fall Day .... Page 110

see: leaves
taste: cider
hear: leaves crunching
feel: cool air
smell: apples (or cider)

A Trip to the Farm .... Page 111

1. A
2. D
3. B
4. C

Sharing .... Page 112

1. A
2. C
3. C
4. A

A Strange Meeting .... Page 113

1. Yes
2. No
3. Yes
4. No

A Day Off .... Page 114

1. C
2. A
3. B
4. C

At the Beach .... Page 115

1. C
2. A
3. B
4. E
5. D

Riding Bikes .... Page 116

1. C
2. A
3. A
4. B

Learning About Bees .... Page 117

Clean hive
Take care of baby bees
Fan wings
Get nectar

The Lost Pet .... Page 118

1. T
2. F
3. F
4. T

Animal Friends .... Page 119

1. B
2. B
3. C
4. C

Lunch Time .... Page 120

1. B
2. B
3. C
4. A

Trisha's Pet .... Page 121

1. B
2. A
3. C
4. A

A News Story .... Page 122

1. C
2. B
3. C
4. A